GHOSTWRITING

Also in The Paragon House Writer's Series

HOW TO PREPARE YOUR MANUSCRIPT FOR A
PUBLISHER
David L. Carroll

A MANUAL OF WRITER'S TRICKS
David L. Carroll

Forthcoming

THE FILMWRITER'S FORMAT BOOK
Rick Reichman

WRITING AND SELLING MAGAZINE ARTICLES
Eva Shaw

THE WRITER'S BOOK OF CONTRACTS
Karen Zubin

GHOSTWRITING

HOW TO GET INTO THE BUSINESS

Eva Shaw

PARAGON HOUSE
New York

The sample agreements and contracts contained in this book are for your information only. All legal matters should be referred to an attorney. You should consult your lawyer before adopting any contract or agreement in this book.

The cases and examples cited in this book are based on actual situations and people. Names and identifying details have been changed to protect privacy.

First edition, 1991

Published in the United States by

Paragon House
90 Fifth Avenue
New York, NY 10011

Manufactured in the United States of America
10 9 8 7 6 5 4 3 2 1

Library of Congress Cataloging-in-Publication Data
Shaw, Eva, 1947–
    Ghostwriting : how to get into the business / Eva Shaw.— 1st ed.
        p.   cm.
    Includes bibliographical references (p. 175).
    ISBN 1–55778–373–X
    1. Ghostwriting.   2. Authorship—Collaboration.
3. Authorship—Marketing.   I. Title.
PN171.G47S5   1991
808'.02—dc20   90-19485
                                                                CIP

Dedication

To ———————— (ghost, please add your name in enormous letters): You put your ego aside to perform an invaluable service, write brilliant words, produce wonderful copy, and work harder than anyone believes is humanly possible.

To all future ghosts ———————— (add your name here): Ghostwriting is the best of all writing professions. To take the first steps to a sensational career, read this book. AND keep one sentence in mind: If you want business, ask for it.

Dedication

Contents

Acknowledgments

A SPECIAL thank-you to all the clients who have trusted me with their books, articles, columns, speeches, you name it. As your ghost, I want to reach out and clasp your hands in gratitude. But I won't tell the world that I am your printed voice.

As this book idea came full circle from a concept to a full-blown manuscript, many have encouraged me. From the very first my husband Joe was more than supportive for a book on ghostwriting: the spirited business. While he admits to not being able to keep up with my ghostwriting clients' names or professions, he'll always be my number one fan.

Throughout the writing process and my colorful (to say the least) career as a ghost, family and friends have constantly lent an ear and a red pencil to manuscripts when necessary. Sometimes they rally to my causes; sometimes they laugh at anecdotal stories. I'm exceedingly fortunate to have a son who understands that my career choice is hardly a nine-to-five job, a comrade who really listens and speaks from her mind and her heart, and wonderful friends and associates who give me freedom to be a friend, a writer, and a ghost simultaneously.

My agent (the world's best) Bert Holtje had the finesse to bring this concept to the attention of Paragon House and deserves another round of applause. And my Paragon House editor PJ Dempsey and her assistant Christopher O'Connell must be acknowledged . . . they've done a magnificent job of tightening and targeting my words to motivate and inform you, the reader.

No effort is singular . . . thank you all.

Introduction

MOST ghostwriters are hired to write books; therefore that's where my emphasis will lie. But that's not all a ghostwriter does. Some specialize in one area, say how-to articles for experts, yet most ghosts make a living writing in a multitude of fields from speeches to advertisements.

The same how-to instruction covered here throughout holds true for ghostwriting books as well as magazine and newspaper stories, brochures, or pamphlets. You can make a great living ghosting these types of material, yet they are considered smaller jobs. Normally they're done for a flat fee on a work-for-hire basis. The ghostwriter may or may not get a byline and will not usually receive any royalties.

I recently wrote a ten-page workbook on estate planning for a local attorney who practices elder law. I acquired this client through the methods discussed in chapter 3. He and I negotiated a set amount when work began; he paid one-half the fee before I started and the second portion when I turned the final copy and computer disk over to his office staff. My name did not appear on the workbook. This was a "quicky" job for which I was paid over one thousand dollars and it fit well between other long-term contracted ghostwriting on book projects. It also led to the attorney hiring me to ghostwrite a monthly column for a seniors' newsletter and a great referral to a very promising client.

While we'll talk about writing books, if you're currently working on a series of booklets or columns, exchange the word book for your project. The information is just as valid.

Now, let's get started.

Part One

BECOMING
A
GHOSTWRITER

CHAPTER
1

Getting into the Business

1.1 Ghost for Hire

Ghostwriters or ghosts make their living assisting, writing for, and collaborating with professionals, scientists, actors, hookers, the rich, the not-so-rich, and anyone else who has something to say.

Why do clients hire a ghostwriter? Reasons include:

1. The client may not have the talent to write.
2. The client may not have the skills, energy, or organizational aptitude to complete a project.
3. The client may not have the time to write.
4. The client may realize writing is a craft and more efficient, marketable, productive, and effective when undertaken by a professional.
5. The client may be a great writer, but simply doesn't want to write a particular book or project.

There's no mystery about ghostwriters. They are a professional group of hard-working writers, who have a sharper-than-average ability to write in the distinct voice of their client. Sounds impossible? Not so . . . it is an art that can be learned.

All it takes to become a ghostwriter is the ability to put your ego aside (at least while writing for a client), study his or her word pattern, have perfect communication with the client, and be an expert in people skills. Of course it helps if you write for money and pleasure, enjoy stimulating conversation, have a great sense of humor and an even disposition, and can keep your wits while the world seems to be going mad.

Why ghost? Ghostwriting is profitable. It's a creative area with growth potential and freedom of choice. Yet at times it is snubbed and/or ignored by freelancers.

The operative word here is *profitable.* Money. Savings accounts. Investments. Financial freedom. Imagine endorsing checks and depositing writing money into your account. Yes, there is excellent money to be made because ghostwriting is a gold mine for an industrious, creative, practical, and energetic writer.

Ghostwriting is a skill, make no mistake. However, to do it for a living, it takes a writer with common sense. When you consider the rewards as a boost to your own writing career, you can easily stand back and be thankful that not every writer wants to do this.

How do ghosts make money and save their self-esteem? By keeping it business. A professional ghostwriter provides a service, producing informational and entertaining words in a timely manner, and leaving the client free to pursue his or her career field. The client has full control over the copy and the ghostwriter is paid by the client, company, or publisher for services rendered and arranged before the writing begins.

1.2   More Here Than Meets the Page

In our service-oriented society, ghostwriting is just that . . . a service many professionals use because written communication isn't their forte or they don't have time. As a ghost, you may not get the glory, but ghostwriting can sizzle your career. People may not hound you for autographs, but they will want you to write for them.

What follows is an overview of material that can be ghostwritten. Once you acquire the knack to know there's a ghost involved, you'll discover even more options for your work.

Ghostwritten work can include novels, short stories, confession stories, plus everything in nonfiction from medical reports and self-help to alternative life-style and travel. Other areas are autobiographies and history as well as motivational material from the latest communications guru. Pop psychology and textbooks are also often ghosted, and diet doctors and exercise experts would hardly make a move without a writer by their side. Memoirs, adventure tales, as-told-to experiences, inspirational books, sex manuals, political reports, and definitely kiss-and-tell tomes finish this short list. To recap: nonfiction, fiction, short stories, articles, newsletters, radio scripts, speeches, and reports, to name a few. The areas where your ghostwriting talents could be used would fill this book and beyond; the above is just to whet your interest.

The fundamental characteristics of successful ghost-writers are 1) that they can do a number of different projects with speed, quality, and accuracy, and 2) that they are flexible enough to change the focus of a project midstream, or stop to put energy into another concept if necessary.

1.3   Twenty Reasons to Become a Ghost

1. *For the challenge.* You'll have to stretch your capabilities further than you may think humanly possible. Right now you might think you know about dogs—there's one in your backyard and you trained her not to jump on guests. But if you ghosted a book for a nationally known cocker spaniel trainer, you'd have to dig through volumes on canine physiology, pet psychology, veterinary medicine, the breeding, feeding, and meeting habits of cockers, and interview various experts in the field. You'd end up becoming somewhat of an expert yourself. But as a ghost, that would only be one field in which you'd have knowledge.

2. *To extend your own knowledge.* You'll be asked to write on subjects you formerly may have thought incomprehensible—perhaps from irradiated food and its effect on Third World nations to the life

cycle of a tadpole. Do you know your way around reference books? Do you know how to ask questions that elicit information? Can you extract pertinent data and keep the remainder from confusing your own brain and that of your reader? Can you translate technical material into words that will inform, not put the reader to sleep?

3. *To hone your skills.* As a ghost, your skill as a writer will get an on-the-job fine tuning, while someone else is paying for the tune-up. Could you take a bare-bones idea—say on the topic of telephone courtesy—and transform it into a book written for customer service reps employed by an insurance company . . . and make it fun to read?

4. *To give yourself credit where it's due.* You have to be a better-than-average writer to ghost because you must adapt your writer's voice to the client's. However, you must also promote yourself and speak up about your skills so the world knows you are there . . . for hire.

5. *To extend your credentials.* Close your eyes and concentrate on seeing your name become a household word . . . or known as the writer of those celebrity books lining the bookstore shelves. What would satisfy you? Money, a contribution to humanity, a fat nest egg, calling an editor by his or her first name? Ghostwriting is the key to many doors.

6. *For the money to live on while your own project, novel, nonfiction book is written and sold.* Ghostwriting can give you capital and the inspiration to work on

your own in an even more dedicated way since your extra time will now be somewhat limited. But depending on your agreement with the client, you may be able to use some of the material from your ghostwriting project as sources for possible articles about your client or related topics.

7. *For the love of writing.* Writing is an affair of the heart. It's the feel of words as they fly through your brain, your fingers connecting with the keyboard as an entire page appears on the computer screen. It's seeing a reader's face, knowing you've provided information and/or entertainment, knowing you've reformatted complex facts into easy-to-comprehend terms. Writing is passionate and addictive and by ghostwriting, you can have the opportunity to do even more of it.

8. *For regular pay up to an extraordinary income.* How much would you really like to earn? How much will it take to keep life and limb together? Ghostwriting can be a regular job . . . just like being a teacher or a secretary. It can also be normal, count-on income and can lead you to new possibilities that skyrocket your earning power.

9. *To have flexibility in your career.* Ghostwriting can be a fantastic part-time career or you can do it twelve months a year. As a ghost, you can make your own schedule, build a house, trek around Bulgaria, see junior get a merit badge . . . or even not write. You call the shots every day.

10. *For the satisfaction of ultimately being your own boss . . . with your own business.* You're in charge. You can make or break your chances for success because you're the CEO. Every drop of sweat is for you and your future.

11. *For the pleasure of writing about provocative, dynamic, and exotic people.* Stop feeling like a potential keyhole peeper; you may not be hired as a professional snoop or even anything close to it. Not all books are the intimate confessions of movie stars. There are zillions of fine, respectable athletes, astronauts, and archaeologists who need to share their tales, too.

12. *To chronicle the history makers of yesterday, today, and tomorrow.* All those important people who make a difference are potential clients for your ghostwritten material. What you write and how you write it can have a positive or negative impact on history.

13. *To promote the personalities you respect and admire.*

14. *To change the image of something or someone who's received bad press.* Let your ghostwritten words educate others or at least give them something to think about. Words have power. As a ghost, you can sway public opinion.

15. *To promote products, causes, charities, businesses, or personal vendettas.* These include saving the wildlife on the lake in your county; getting your community's government to place a crossing guard in

front of the elementary school; helping a local merchant write newsletters, brochures, and press releases to promote his or her business.

16. *To right a wrong; to clarify or promote a timely issue.* Your ghostwriting skills could be needed in public relations . . . or for public officials or community residents.

17. *To record a family history or detail a dynasty.* Violet-perfumed Grandma Philpot of Philadelphia might not seem like a potential client for a ghost-written book; however, look again. There's a trend for matriarchs to record their private memoirs to share and inspire this generation of career women . . . and those memories must be recorded before they are lost forever. Writing family histories, memoirs, autobiographies and biographies could be your bread and butter . . . if you have the talent to help tell tales.

18. *To keep your own privacy.* There may be opportunities that shout career move, but personally the book you'd ghost could potentially embarrass another who is close to you or to a long-established client. Ghosting is the answer.

19. *To extend your marketability.* Ghostwriting for a child psychologist could enable you to learn sound techniques to help your kids . . . but more so, you'll learn tips you can incorporate within future how-to books or articles. And think about this: Ghostwriting for the president would look great

on anyone's resume . . . regardless of political affiliation.

20. *Just for the fun of it.* Ghostwriting is *fun*.

1.4 Do You Have What It Takes to Be a Ghost?

Write *Yes* or *No* to the following questions on the line provided. Total only your *Yes* answers and then compare them with the information at the end of the quiz.

___ 1. Do you have strong, yet thoughtful values?

___ 2. Are you always the one who leads a discussion?

___ 3. Is your motto: Two heads are better?

___ 4. Do you get angry or even slightly upset when asked to revise, edit, or totally dispose of material and start fresh?

___ 5. Can you carry on an articulate conversation with almost anyone?

___ 6. Can you keep on discussion points in a disagreement?

___ 7. Are you intuitive?

___ 8. Can you give and take criticism about your writing and ideas?

___ 9. Can you say no and stick with it?

___ 10. Have you ever successfully asked for a raise?

___ 11. Can you separate fact from emotion?

11

   __ 12. Do you like to find out why people do certain things?

   __ 13. Do you accept that white lies have a place in our society?

The questions are presented to gear your mind toward the alliance of ghostwriting. There are no right or wrong answers; however, if your total of Yes responses is:

Eleven or more. You are flexible and a great candidate as a ghost. However, you may be too accommodating and a client could Sherman Tank you into making judgment errors. Make sure both you and your client understand your specific work roles.

Seven to ten. You could face a few blocks as a ghost. However, your strong opinions and resourcefulness will be beneficial with the right client. Communicate what you need and want in a professional manner.

Six and under. Your opinions and values, that sensitive side of your nature, will make your own work outstanding. If you're serious about becoming a ghost, work on team skills, study the craft, and then do it.

1.5 Scouting Out the Possibilities

At one time ghosts were anonymous . . . even the kiss-and-tell books didn't reveal who helped the kisser or the kissee map the juicy plot. There was a time when celebrities and their publishers alike would have balked at giving credit to ghosts. Movie stars, CEOs, motivational speakers, and athletes wanted the public to believe their expertise went beyond the bedroom, ball field, and board room.

Ghostwriting is no longer a hush-hush profession. It's visible on the front cover of nearly every nonfiction personality-written book on the market. Leo Janos (and Chuck Yeager) wrote *Yeager*, Peter Bonventre (and Howard Cosell) coauthored *I Never Played the Game*, and William Novak (and Lee Iacocca) penned *Iacocca* and (with Nancy Reagan) *My Turn*. There's absolutely no mistaking the change. There was a time when these books would have needed only the celebrity's name. People don't look suspiciously at a coauthor's name anymore; on the contrary, the public realizes not everyone has the talent to organize words.

How many notables use ghostwriters? There's never been a statistic but once you begin looking at the volumes at your bookstore you'll quickly see that it's a growth industry. Corporate heads, starlets, sex symbols, dethroned politicians, doctors, lawyers, Indian chiefs, the Hopes, the DeLoreans, and the Mayflower madams have partners.

On a local level business people, your city's mayor or mayoral candidate, people who have been through a life-threatening experience, people who want to tell the world anything hire a ghost. Are ghostwriters then the worker bees? Perhaps, but as a writer, how would you react if your name was right there on the *New York Times* bestseller list, although in slightly smaller print than the client?

If you're serious about your work, ghosting can only promote your stock in trade . . . a word craft that can take you from mediocre to megabucks.

1.6   The Options of Ghostwriting

You're convinced that ghostwriting is profitable, right? So now the question becomes, why don't more writers take the challenge?

1. *Fear.* As a ghost, you'll have to prove yourself with each undertaking. You'll only be as good as your last book or project. You may have to audition for the part of ghostwriter and unless you have an agent, you'll be required to promote yourself. You'll also have to extend your talent further than you probably thought possible, and immerse yourself in someone's life story, political views, or product appeal, even though they may not really appeal to you.

2. *Enhanced income.* Mike Lupica, who ghosted two books, says he demands between five and one hundred thousand dollars for professional services. Others say they do it for royalties, flat fees, and percentages of royalties. Few do it for love alone.

3. *Negative experiences.* There are ghosts who say they'd never do it again. There's one celebrity who refused to pay, hassled the final work, removed golden words, cut out the marketable parts, plagued the writer with collect calls at midnight, and de-

manded rewrites. However, in the big picture, everyone knows there's a Murphy's Law that says once in a lifetime, everyone is forced to work with someone despicable . . . it happens in a ghostwriter's career too.

4. *Sticky issues.* What happens, if given a free hand on content, moral issues suddenly surface. Everyone has a skeleton in their closet. What if you discover something totally out of the client's character that could drastically alter the way the public visualizes him or her? What would you do if the client absolutely refuses to discuss this? What if you excavate something that could jeopardize the client's reputation or career? What would you do if you discover that his or her research was faulty, backed by nothing more scientific than a verbose hunch? Check your own ethics before you begin.

5. *Plagiarism.* It doesn't exactly run rampant in ghostwriting circles, but what will you do if your client presents some sensational poetry to include in his memoirs? You realize from freshman English that these sonnets sound very familiar and would be better credited to the Bard. Or the diet and exercise research your author wants to include was taken verbatim from a recognized doctor's best-selling book of five years ago?

Fear, income that is variable, and the issue of ethics are part of ghostwriting. All professions have their unwritten obstacles.

CHAPTER
2

The Professional Ghostwriter

2.1 The Complete Ghost

A ghostwriter is a professional. He or she works long hours, keeps accurate records for the IRS, and is serious about the craft.

Most ghostwriters work in an office often within their homes, or at a desk in their client's office. Most ghostwriters work eight to five, and five, six, and at times seven days a week. The ghostwriters who make it are professionals and understand that they'll be privy to innermost particulars of their client's life or business. They must always be discreet. In addition they realize that to continue and receive referrals, they must produce excellent copy. They must meet deadlines while simultaneously projecting their client in the light he or she wishes to appear.

While you may not wear three-piece suits to your office (which may even be a spare bedroom), you will be expected to dress like a professional when working with clients. The clients will take you far more seriously if you do. Like it or not, clothing adds to credibility. However, credibility may be situational. William Novak, while writing Nancy Reagan's book *My Turn*, wore jeans and T-shirts when recording her thoughts at her ranch north of Santa Barbara. When working with Lee Iacocca, Novak dressed like an up-and-coming executive for the executive's brusque no-nonsense approach.

2.2 Your Personal Professional Sales Presentation

Over the telephone, face to face, or through a query letter, you have fifteen seconds to get your point across, sway someone's thinking, promote yourself as a ghostwriter. Fifteen seconds. It's beneficial, therefore, to have your personal sales presentation memorized. Don't mumble something about the fact you write. Have one prepared, have it ready, because everyone you meet is a potential client.

2.3 Using Your Network

If you don't network, you won't do well in ghostwriting. Many successful ghostwriters don't advertise; they obtain plenty of work by referrals . . . getting the word out through their network that they're available (See appendix C).

Join organizations for that distinct purpose and carry

your business cards *at all times* . . . even to the grocery store and the amusement park. Experts in the field of networking estimate that we all know about 250 people . . . not close, personal friends, but we have an acquaintanceship with that many. Multiply that out and you'll be astounded by the figure . . . and each could be a prospective client.

2.4   The Ghostwriter's Image

Your Resume

Depending on the agreement you have with a client, he or she may not want the world at large to know you're the spark behind the sparkling words. Conversely some clients shout the fact they've hired so-and-so to take their ideas and produce them into books, syndicated newspaper columns, and speeches.

If you want to promote yourself, but can't divulge who your clients have been (or are), how can you list them on your resume? Here's how one ghost solves the problem. After an overview of credits under her own byline, she has a paragraph titled:

GHOSTWRITER: Clients include a nationally known physician, a television soap star, a motivational speaker, an NFL coach, a health expert, a romance novelist, and a retired military specialist. Publication of clients' work includes *USA Today*, the *Los Angeles Times Magazine*,

Woman's Day, *American Health*, *Shape Magazine*, plus more than two hundred other books, magazine articles, and newspaper columns, in addition to newsletters, press releases, speeches, and reports.

This format assures the confidentiality of each client. Should a potential client want to know details, the ghost contacts the reference, asks for permission to give his or her name, and then supplies the particulars including telephone number, address, and a convenient time to contact the reference.

If your clients agree, do list their names and the types of projects you've completed.

And if you haven't worked as a ghost before? Absolutely don't lie. Publishing is a very intimate community and you'll be found out. Your resume should list professional writing credentials, the areas of your expertise, and the fact that you are a ghostwriter.

As with other professional resumes, list your published credits, professional background, pertinent degrees, and associations and career objectives if appropriate. You may want to break down the categories of your resume into topics such as: GHOSTWRITER, FREELANCE WRITER, LECTURER, AUTHOR, and COLUMNIST.

Some ghosts include professional references; some list other nonwriting information such as other occupations, associations, age, and marital status. A few ghosts have their resumes printed with a photo of themselves at the top.

Basically it's best to stick with a professional image for

your resume: white paper, no typos, excellent format. If you're in doubt about what's contemporary and suitable, the public library has plenty of reference books on preparing resumes. Have it prepared and ready so that when asked for samples of your work, your resume can be clipped to them.

Business Cards and Stationery

Although it's not absolutely imperative to have printed letterhead stationery with matching envelopes, it does give you a professional edge . . . and sometimes that's all a potential client will see. You may want to use the various printing fonts on your computer to design letterhead; doing it yourself cuts an initial expense, but make it look as tasteful as possible.

Along with stationery business cards are invaluable . . . use them generously even if it feels awkward at first. Your business card is a personal advertisement; don't hesitate to enclose one with query letters.

If you have cards and stationery and envelopes printed, steer clear of the exotic; they'll remember your scorching pink business cards, but you won't be thought of as a trusted writer.

The Telephone

Part of your image is the way in which you answer the telephone. A client may or may not care where you conduct business, whether it's the card table that you call your desk or an office in your home. Yet by answering in an upbeat business manner such as, "Good morning, this is Mary Smith," the client immediately knows he or she has dialed the correct number, knows to whom he or she is speaking, and most importantly that you are serious in your role as a ghostwriter, ready and eager to devote attention to the client's needs.

The client really doesn't need to know that you've just bathed the baby and are standing dripping wet balancing the tot and the phone. Don't divulge that fact. Communicate as a proficient writer perhaps sitting at your walnut desk, seriously perusing the thesaurus, just waiting for that call, and you're accepted as a professional.

Keep in mind that the tone and words you choose and how you're received on the other end of the telephone can have a positive or negative impact on your business. If you have an accent that you dislike, take some diction lessons. If you routinely use the same slang words as your teenager, eradicate them from your vocabulary including the ah and uh sounds. And if you normally use even mild swear words, in most cases you'll be thought less professional.

Smile when you talk, make your voice sound overjoyed that the client is calling, take notes when talking, follow through with what you've said you'll do . . . and you'll succeed. If you have any doubts about how you sound, tape-record your voice reading a few paragraphs. You may consciously want to lower your pitch and slow your speech so that you can be easily understood. Ask a trusted friend to critique your telephone manner.

Depending on your household, you may require a separate line with an answering machine for your office. When designing your telephone message, speak clearly with a firm tone. Make your message warm, sincere, and inviting, but businesslike. Control the noise in the background; say your name and telephone number slowly. Here's an example:

> This is Jack Jones. The number you've reached is 555-1212. I'm sorry I missed your call; it's important to me. Will you please leave your name, telephone number, time, date, and why you've called. I'll return your call shortly. Thank you.

When you're required to leave messages, be sure to speak clearly and slowly. You may want to spell your name, even if it's a simple one, and give the digits of your phone number precisely.

Return messages promptly. If the caller isn't in suggest a time that's convenient for you (and when you'll be in the office) and you won't have to play telephone tag.

2.5   References: How to Get Them and Keep Them Happy

As with any other instance when you give someone's name as a professional reference, be sure to obtain permission first. The references you list on a resume must attest to your skill as a ghostwriter. In addition your references should have had personal experience with your knowledge, ability to meet deadlines, and your work. Remember, too, to be confidential in your dealings.

Initially as a ghostwriter you may want to list editors of magazines for whom you've worked and colleagues, associates, or professors who know your writing.

Your reference list, as with your resume, will need updating often as you garner more impressive credits.

CHAPTER
3

How to Begin

3.1   Attracting Clients

For those of us who make money as writers, ghostwriting began as a viable thought, turned into a part-time profession, and then became a full-time job as clients told others about how they "found" the perfect person to write for them.

When you begin you'll have to tell everyone you know that you're a ghostwriter . . . explain what a ghost does and how you can, as a ghost, do whatever your prospective client does with the written word, only better. This all must be accomplished without sounding even slightly egotistical . . . and can be done by stressing the practicality of utilizing the services of ghosts. In order to attract clients you must become an opportunist. Seek out situations where someone might need a ghostwriter. You cannot be shy. As a ghost you must speak up for yourself, talk about your profession, and have your personal sales presentation ready at all times.

Ask your current clients to refer you. Ask the editors of

magazines you've worked with, your literary agent, the editor of your local paper, the reference librarian at the public library to give out your name as a ghost for hire. Potential clients are apt to ask book-oriented people if they know someone who writes for compensation. And that's when your foot gets in the door.

As an opportunist, look at every piece of junk mail that hits your mailbox, especially those from local companies and professionals. As an opportunist, keep your ears and eyes open for seminars and workshops in your area given by anyone who has anything to sell or promote. As an opportunist, contact individuals who have recently been awarded some honor, been publicized in the newspaper, accepted an office. These are all possible clients.

3.2   Advertising

Advertising is expensive. You must wait for someone to find your ad, and then you must sort out the serious from the curious. But advertising isn't always the best method.

So what's a ghost to do when advertising doesn't generate serious clients? Format a multifaceted marketing campaign, one that may include traditional advertising avenues such as writers' magazines, *Publishers Weekly*, national newspapers, local papers. If money is tight, look to active advertising by joining networking groups, service groups, organizations, whether it's the Sierra Club or the Young Democrats.

Active advertising also means you can publicize your-self. Local newspapers, magazines, and advertising tab-loids love articles about locals making good. And your rags-to-riches story would make a wonderful, inspira-tional tale. When you've accomplished something, write and send out press releases to the local media. As your own PR firm you must tell the media you're a ghostwriter and you'd make a great personality profile for their pub-lication. Offer to teach local groups the secrets of effective writing, design a writing class for the community col-lege, give workshops to service groups like Rotary . . . all designed to get your name out in the newspaper. Your local newspaper and college catalogue are excellent *free* advertising—make sure you tell the paper and college to refer telephone queries. And for fun answer ads in the classified sections of metropolitan newspapers under the listings for writers and editors.

When calls, letters, and referrals come, always follow through, even if they initially look like a waste of time. Call or write the prospective client immediately and send a copy of your resume and samples of your work. Offer to meet at a convenient time and place to discuss the project. Take the initiative . . . you're an opportunist.

Some ghosts charge a consulting fee for the initial meeting and they expect payment of the fee that day, most probably the result of too many exhausting, non-productive encounters. I screen potential clients over the telephone and realize that the initial meeting is to my benefit in order to size up the client as well as discuss the project.

With all referrals, make a point of sending a thank-you note to the individual who gives you the referral and you'll receive more. Referrals are a two-way street. Be sure to pass on work that isn't in your area to other writers.

3.3   Doing Your Homework

There's absolutely nothing worse than talking with a potential client and feeling as if you've left your brain at home. In order to make the most of every meeting you must do your homework.

Homework can consist of searching out past issues of a newspaper for information on a client, reading what has been written about or by him or her, talking with others who know the client, or doing some quick research on the topic that he or she wants to write about.

If you're meeting a client who wants to write about growing up in Italy during the early forties, for example, you'd better search out information on Mussolini and the Fascist form of government, and review the years that war raged in Italy . . . especially if all you know about Italy is food, shoes, and Sophia Loren.

If the client you're meeting has had things written about him or her, including academic or scientific books and papers, it behooves you to be familiar at least with the content and titles. It's flattering to tell the prospective client, "I enjoyed the article about you in *USA Today* and admire your zeal for Oriental art." Firstly, the client knows you took time to find out something more than a credit rating or where he or she lives. And secondly, you can begin your conversation with some comfortable small talk on a common area, thus making everyone feel more comfortable.

Which brings up a point you may not have considered: anxiety. Your client is probably more anxious about this meeting than you. You've worked with and will work with many clients who want to hire a ghost. You talk about writing to your family and friends—there's no mystery about what you do for a living to anyone who is close to you. However, this may be the only time your prospective client will ever hire anyone to write his or her words. It's expensive, it's putting that delicate ego on the line, and it's new. All three add up to anxious feelings that you can help alleviate by doing your homework, by talking in quietly, competent terms, and by being above-board in all your dealings.

3.4 Meeting Prospective Clients for the First Time

The dress-for-success rules of a navy suit, white blouse or shirt, and red scarf or tie are no longer required. Make yourself look the most professional possible.

Take your tools, definitely another resume (resumes get misplaced or you might suddenly meet another potential client and need an extra), more samples of your work—

perhaps books or lengthy projects you've written under your own name or ghosted—a pen, and a tablet. Fold them well into a clean attaché case.

After setting the appointment write a note or call the day before to confirm it; you'll come across as efficient and serious. It could also save you travel time, frustration, and/or disappointment. Get directions if necessary and carry a map. Have change ready for the valet, parking meter, or pay phone. Allow plenty of time to get to the appointment . . . you do not want to start your relationship with an excuse as to why you are late.

Because you may work out of your house, it's not always feasible to meet in your office, nor appropriate to discuss a project with a client sitting around your kitchen table. Solve this problem by meeting a client, at least initially, in the client's office, a restaurant, or a quiet corner of the public library or by renting a small meeting room in a hotel.

Most people find it preferable to meet in a neutral place. Depending on the project, and as you meet over a nonthreatening cup of coffee, you can mentally go through a checklist to ascertain if you'll be compatible. (See below for specific tips.) Then, because you've met away from your office, when it's time to leave you can glance at your watch, excusing yourself far more easily than if he or she has settled into your couch to give you the intimate details of the last seventy years of a somewhat uneventful life.

Do not feel you'll be branded as a novice if you schedule

more than one meeting with a possible client. It is mandatory that you be comfortable with the client and the project, and snap decisions can spell catastrophe. Every ghost is different, but the following are a few red flags that should make you aware of possible pitfalls in a relationship:

• The client is late (more than once and without a valid excuse).

• The client is overbearing, talking without allowing you to interject information or questions into the dialogue.

• The client doesn't offer any information and every word must be extracted from his or her mouth.

• The client has trouble 1) making initial and pleasant small talk, and/or 2) staying on the topic you've come to discuss, that is, his or her hiring you to be a ghost.

• The client forgets your name, that you're a professional, and/or that your time is valuable.

• The client insists that you make up your mind whether or not you want to work on the book or article at that very first meeting or he or she will find someone else.

• The client balks when you discuss money or pales when you explain your hourly rate.

These red flags *do not* mean that you should not accept the project, only that you need to recognize potential danger areas.

3.5   What to Ask

The potential client will want to ask you many questions including the cost of your writing the project and your availability, background, and experience. This first meeting is crucial for you to decide if you are compatible with this job, so you may want to help your prospective client by offering this information yourself.

The following are some points to cover in the first meeting. There are no right responses. It's up to you to decide after hearing the answers, listening between the statements, and using all of your intuition if this is the project for you. Jot down your questions, then ask the potential client:

1. **Why are you hiring a ghost?** Most will say because they don't have the talent or time to write the book or accomplish the task.
2. **What is your goal for the book/project?** Some will admit it is to make a million dollars; some will say for the satisfaction of sharing their information with the world. Only you can decide if you feel comfortable with the answer.
3. **What money, notoriety, power do you hope to receive?** Watch their faces on this one. Money is wonderful, it allows us choices in life, but ethically speaking if your potential client is a little old woman living on a meager pension, you may want to turn her down if she must pay you from her life savings.

4. **What type of working arrangement do you visualize with a ghostwriter?** Some ghosts prefer working closely with clients; others want plenty of elbowroom, with specific meeting times for collaboration, research, fact approval, and approval of the material. Normally it's best to have a meeting schedule included in the contract. (See Part 2, for information on your ghostwriting agreement.)

5. **Specifically on the book/project, how far along are you in the process, that is, an idea, a series of tapes, research completed, book outlined, manuscript partially written, manuscript finished in draft form?** May I review your material? There's absolutely nothing wrong with a client who wants to start with an idea and have a book written as long as you feel you can deliver the work. Fake it as far as you can, but only promise what you can sincerely accomplish.

6. **Have you worked with other writers?** In what capacity? This is an extremely important question, whether you decide to ask the others or not. If the answer is yes . . . you'll want to find out about the success of those relationships and may want to give this client a wide berth. Normally when you hear a client bad-mouth previous writers, it's a red flag for problems with the client.

7. **Whom do you see as the audience for this book/project?** Many clients never stop to consider that they must direct the material to a specific

audience. Asking this question helps determine if the client's goals are realistic. I prefer visualizing a typical reader and writing for that person.

8. **How much do you have budgeted for the book/ project?** That's a euphemism for how much they will be willing to spend. When we get into chapter 4, Money for Words, we'll talk about how to estimate, but you need to find out, right up front and as tactfully as possible, if your potential client is willing to pay for your services.

9. **Exactly what do you, the client, want from a ghostwriter?** Does the client want you to write the entire book? Edit it for grammar mistakes? Cut the manuscript? Improve the dialogue? Add research?

While clearing misconceptions about your role on the book/project, you may want to talk about the business of publishing. You must be clear about clients' expectations. Does he or she plan to self-publish? To have you write a proposal for agents? Does he or she already have a publishing contract?

As a ghostwriter, you may feel the book will never sell, but that doesn't mean this is true. It's acceptable to make a rule that you'll only ghost books/projects that are already contracted with a major publishing house, but there may come a time when you'll be asked to write (rewrite, edit, etc.) a project you think is absolute rubbish.

At that time, you must ask a few private questions of yourself:

- Can the client afford my services?
- Am I being paid enough?
- Will I be able to sleep at night if I don't personally agree with the content?
- Do I believe in the project enough to invest the time even though it might not "work"?
- Do I know when, professionally, it's best to say no?

On the average of twice a month, I get calls from people who want me to invest time, expertise, and money in their projected writing work. They feel they're doing me an honor by allowing me to write about them. Sometimes the project sounds intriguing; sometimes it's outlandish. I am a working ghostwriter with financial obligations and a future in the profession. Personally I've made a rule that I only work for professional wages. I do not work for free or on future shares as an investment in someone else's career. Yes, there's a possibility I miss something with fantastic promise, but I'm also able to eat and pay my bills.

3.6   The Making of a Marriage: The Client/Ghost Relationship

Consider additional areas to make sure you can have a successful ghost/client relationship. It is a partnership, a business deal, yet a ghostwriter will know details about a client that few people know. While you won't be expected to stay close for years, you will need to decide the following for yourself:

1. Do you respect this person? It sounds old-fashioned but could you work for and with an individual whom you don't respect?
2. How committed is the individual to the project? Has he or she considered doing this for years, or is it something decided on now that ski season is over?
3. Will you honestly and truly feel comfortable working with this person? Will you feel comfortable being introduced as his or her writer? Does the potential client respect your expertise?
4. What's your gut-level feeling about the working relationship? Don't skip this point . . . your response is critical. Realize, here and now, that there will be times when you want a client's work (and the money), but you know in your heart that if you take on the job, you'll feel disturbed. Is the trade off worth it?

Your relationship with your client, unlike a love match, is made on earth, with human conflicts and anxieties. Be honest with yourself and your clients and the relationships will be successful.

3.7   Clients: Working with One or Many

Depending on the other bread-and-butter work you do while ghostwriting, you may only be able to handle writing for one client at a time. If it's a major book project, you will need to devote considerable energy, talent, and time to the project.

However, most ghostwriters have a number of clients, many of whom are working on books, but the books are all at different phases, say a proposal, first draft, or negotiating with a publisher. If you're the type of person who can handle numerous projects at one time, take the plunge and accept more than one ghostwriting client. The trick is staying organized, budgeting your time, and scheduling realistic deadlines.

Never hesitate to be candid with clients about your workload. It's complimentary to know that their ghost has also been hired by others. Your talents are in demand, which indicates you produce excellent work. Also if you're in a lull, you needn't make excuses; instead stress the positive aspect of being free. "I'm just finishing one project and will be available to start your work this afternoon," or, "I'll always make time for your projects, Ms. Jones. I can begin right after we meet on Tuesday."

3.8   Working with Agents and Publishers

Some clients will already have an agent and/or publisher for his or her work when you meet. To avoid a conflict of interest or a potentially awkward situation, find out initially if the agent or publisher knows about you. It will smooth out the process if everyone is truthful because as a professional you can elicit detailed, technical information to make the book/project easier to produce.

One ghost, who's working with a doctor on a book on chemical dependency, acknowledged as a research assistant. It's okay with the ghost and the doctor, but being an assistant instead of a writer might not be okay with you. Give it some thought. If your client prefers to keep you a secret, you'll have to decide if this is acceptable.

Today more than three-quarters of the country's ghostwriters work on a team with the client, agent, and publisher. Because a writer's talents are critical for a salable manuscript, a publisher or agent may ask you to audition for the part of the client's ghost. Be prepared to submit samples of your work to the client's agent or publisher, to discuss the project in detail, and to tell exactly how you'll contribute to the project.

Part Two

THE
BUSINESS
OF
GHOSTWRITING

CHAPTER
4

Money for Words

4.1   Money Is the Issue

For most of us in the writing trade that folding green is a basic necessity of life whether we admit it or not. And at this very second money may be the only reason you're considering ghostwriting as a profession. What's wrong with money as a motive? Nothing.

Make no mistake; there are no constants, no rules to ghostwriting. It's a gut-level, every-writer-for-his-or-herself profession. But there are intelligent ways to succeed and earn a steady income. Ghostwriters normally work for *a flat fee* (such as a work-for-hire arrangement), *on royalties*, or on an *hourly rate*.

After you've reviewed the project, it's wise to discuss your proposed fee with your client and put it in writing. He or she may have to clear the project with another person and a written quote again announces your professionalism.

4.2   Working for a Flat Fee

Work completed for a flat fee is also known as work for hire. In this case, the ghostwriter works as a contractor, does not maintain any copyrights, and once the project is finished, in theory, both the writer and the client bid adieu.

You may be offered a flat fee when your client wants to publish the book him- or herself and take all the credit and incur all the costs. It'll make life easier for you both if you decide on a dollar amount ahead of time, sign an agreement, and go with it rather than work out a royalty agreement.

A flat fee is the preferred choice of some ghostwriters who work with many clients. When a writer enters into an agreement to divide royalties for the life of the book, the writer and the client are forever tied together (unless the agreement is officially dissolved). When they pass on, their estates are tied together. This superglue can be great . . . bringing in tidy little sums, but it's also a time-consuming financial responsibility for the client, the writer, and the publisher to keep track of those sums throughout the years.

Another instance when you may want to work on a flat fee is when you estimate that there will be little use for the end product once it's delivered to the client. A speech for your local congressional representative will be yesterday's news twenty minutes after it's delivered. A book with limited appeal, but with an extremely enthusiastic author (who desperately needs your ghosting talents), may be a more sensible project if you work on a flat fee.

Working for hire—receiving a certain amount of money—can be tricky to estimate, but it's essential that you evaluate what it will take to write this book (project, article, report, speech, catalogue, or ad copy). To determine the flat fee or see if you can live with the one offered consider the following:

How Much Has Been Completed?

Does your client have all the notes professionally double-spaced in chronological order in a three-ring binder? Is the manuscript in rough form? Is it available on a floppy disk compatible with your computer?

Before your mouth even suggests a "Yes, I'll do the book," look over all the material, read it, take your time. If the client will not give you access to everything, review a major sampling.

(Off the record, some novice authors—who will at one time or another turn out to be your clients—feel their words will be stolen if they allow anyone to see or read their material before a contract is signed. It's entirely up to you on how to proceed if this situation arises. You must use your best instincts along with the information you received during your initial meeting to make a decision, if you want to work with the individual.)

As you review the material, ask your client:

43

- Does this typify all the material?
- How many pages have been completed?
- What part of your life (technique, research, information, experience) does this include?

This is not a foolproof system but will give you insight on your client's devotion to detail and how much material you'll have to extract through personal interviews and research.

Don't feel the necessity to make a snap decision. If you have the opportunity take the notes, chapter, or manuscript back to your office in order to estimate a flat fee. While reviewing the material, and strictly for your own edification, rewrite five to fifty pages. You should not give these pages to the client, unless you're feeling extremely benevolent or the work is too sensational to keep to yourself.

This is a test to see if 1) you like working from the client's material, 2) you can do the work, and 3) you have the time it takes to rewrite, polish, and produce the best writing possible. If it takes two days to revise ten pages, you'd better make darn sure your client understands the costs and time involved.

From Your Experience, Would You Buy This Completed Book?

Think business. For example, your potential client wants to write about the cabin cruiser he designed on the coast of Maine one summer when he was twelve. The chances of the book being a megabucks hit are far slim-mer if he's an orthodontist from Oroville than if he's the dashing young captain who has just won back the Amer-ica's Cup and whose face is appearing on television com-mercials plugging everything from chewing gum to Disneyland.

Will You Need to Interview Personal Sources?

That may include a high school chemistry teacher or the movie star's ex-lover . . . you name it and he or she could be on the list. Who will provide the names, phone numbers, and access to the interviewees? Will you make the call, will your client introduce you, or will a secretary prepare an introduction?

Will He or She Supply the Resource Information?

This point could cut your time down considerably, especially if the book is on a subject with which you are totally unfamiliar. Will you be given the research mate-rial, or will you have to dig it out?

Will You Tape Your Time Together?

Will you be expected to write it down in longhand or will the client dictate the outline for you to fill in? Who will transcribe the tapes? Can you understand the client's voice on the tape?

Will You Be Able to Work on a Regular Schedule or During a Predetermined Number of Hours Per Week?

Will that be convenient for both of you? This is not the time to gloss over the fact that you may have to relocate to Seattle for a month.

Will You Be Required to Travel, Make Long-Distance Phone Calls, or Spend Time in the Client's Office to Get the Feel of Your Client's Personality?

Will you be reimbursed? Who will pay for the airline fare, hotel bill, or cat food while you're away? And when will you be paid for these out-of-pocket expenses?

What Is the Deadline for the Book/Project?

Will you have enough time to do a professional job? How will the book work in with other projects to which you're currently committed?

Once you get the feel for these issues you'll understand that you just can't say that since the manuscript is estimated to be sixty thousand words and you normally charge ten cents a word for books, the fee will be six thousand dollars. For instance, after reviewing a plum project you learn you must travel to Detroit (in the dead of December). You'll need to buy appropriate clothing for below-freezing temperatures including wooly long johns for a stay in a hotel for three months while working with the client. You'll also have to do things like drive to Lansing from Motown every other day. You'll probably end up in the red if you take the job with these specifications and without being reimbursed. By all means be honest with your client about your concerns. Money is a consideration for the client, too.

You may want to assemble all the pluses and minuses of the book in a list, discuss the risks privately with a trusted advisor, and only then make a decision.

4.3 Working for Royalties

As you become better known as a ghost, clients will come to you and offer to share the profits from their books. Review the questions above before you give the client an answer. And before you nod your head, research the topic and consider the competition. Look at the marketability of the project and remember you'll be locked in a legal agreement with the person for quite a while . . . a lifetime, that is.

Working strictly for royalties can be quite a gamble, like playing the horses or the lottery, or deciding whether to kiss on the first date. Risks, however, are cut by obtaining more data. William Novak (*Iacocca*) accepted a flat fee reported to be about fifty thousand dollars for writing the Chrysler king's memoirs. With bonuses, his total grew to be about eighty thousand. That is only a fraction of what he could have earned if he'd chosen to work on a 15 percent royalty basis. Moneywise, it didn't work out that great for Novak, but reputationwise the career move to write for Lee changed Novak's future to the plus side as the hottest ghost in the business. *Time* magazine recently called him "the golden mouthpiece of American celebrities."

If you're interested in royalties and if the book project resembles a sure thing, consider a fee and royalties . . . and have it nicely assembled in a legal agreement. Be wary of possible clients and collaborators who want you to invest money in their books. Remember your time *is* money.

4.4   Working on an Hourly Rate

On smaller projects, for example a booklet on posture for the local chiropractor, it may be okay to work at an hourly rate. A new ghostwriter with very limited writing experience may charge fifteen dollars an hour. However, a seasoned professional with a long track record will charge $150 per hour plus expenses.

When working at an hourly rate, you'll still be wise to send a letter of confirmation to your client or work with a statement of intent. If you haven't worked with this client before, ask for a certain amount of your estimated fee up front. Don't feel any shame for doing this sensible businesswise maneuver.

Asking for money is awkward at first, but it gets easier with every asking. Just say, "It's my policy to receive five hours fee, $250.00, before I begin work." Receiving half your fee ahead of time does two things. First, you know the client is serious and second, should the client change his or her mind, you have part of the expected fee, which is better than nothing.

Sorry to break the news, but there are people who will waste your time and energy on wild-goose chases. Of course, you could hire an attorney, take the client to court, contact a collection agency, and charge interest on the unpaid balance. But on small amounts—say under two hundred dollars—the truth is it may be far easier to go on with your life and not make the same mistake again.

4.5 Not-So-Simple Calculations for Ghostwriting Fees

Although you may not get a straight answer, ask other writers, specifically professional ghosts, what they charge. If you preface the question by letting the writer know why you're asking, a fellow author will at least give you a ballpark figure.

If you belong to writers' organizations, such as the National Writers' Club, discuss fees with a member or someone on their staff. Also consider what you'd be paid if you were writing a newspaper story or a magazine article. If you have a full-time job and ghostwrite on the side, how much is your normal pay (excluding benefits)?

When making your calculations consider how long the

project will run. You're selling your time, time which could be spent on your own novel or career, so it's essential that you're satisfied with the deal.

Start with an hourly rate of one hundred dollars (strictly for the sake of argument) and work through the calculations below to give you a beginning amount:

Expected hourly rate (R) multiplied by the number of hours you expect the project to take (T) equals what you'll charge (C) [R × T = C]. Therefore if you charge one hundred dollars an hour and expect the project to take five hours, your estimate should be five hundred.

If you normally write for publications that pay per word, just multiply that figure by the number of proposed words in the project.

There is a catch here. You must be *flexible*. If you know your client isn't independently wealthy but are still willing to undertake the job—whether it's because you believe in the book or need the bucks—do your estimates, make all those calculations, but adapt to the circumstances.

Be realistic as you are flexible. How much could you expect for an advance from a publishing house? Would it be two thousand, four thousand, or fifty thousand dollars? Charging your client the normal twenty cents a word, multiplied by sixty thousand words (which is the proposed length of this book) should, by the formula, increase your bank account by twelve thousand.

Again, be realistic as you are flexible. Each client and project is different . . . there are no sets of absolutes.

As you review the project, think of the marketing possibilities such as selling excerpts from the book to magazines. While you might not make a lot of money, your byline could prove an excellent career boost, especially if the excerpt were in a major national magazine.

Go directly to your agent for advice on how much to charge, if you haven't done so already. If you have no agent, you've got to proceed with your own calculations and your own instinct.

4.6   Fees for Various Ghostwritten Projects

According to a recent not-so-absolute survey of ghostwriters, here is a fee schedule to consider at least as a point of reference. All of the amounts reflect ghostwritten work.

Books: Precontracted 50 to 75 percent of advance plus expenses. Written, with no credit for the ghost's work, $2,500 to $50,000, plus expenses, such as self-published books. Hourly rate on books $25 to $75.

Corporate book/policy manual: $3,000 to $25,000.

Book proposals: $300 to $1000 depending on research involved.

Editing/rewriting: $25 to $50 per hour.

Novel synopsis: $100 to $300 for under ten pages.

Speeches: $25 to $100 per hour, upward scale for political candidates.

Syndicated newspaper column: $50 to $250 for 500 to 750 words.

Textbook writing: $35 to $75 per hour.

Writing for a client: $25 to $100 an hour, plus expenses.

Writing article: $350 to $5000.

Writing for professional (doctor, attorney): $50 to $250 an hour, plus expenses.

4.7 Tips for Living and Earning as a Ghost

Ghostwriters who do it as a full-time job earn from thirty to one hundred thousand dollars a year. These are not the stars who write for the people we see in the news and on television, but real people like you and me. They are creative word pros, people with a flair for writing in another's voice.

If they can do it, you can do it. Here then are some tips to keep motivation high as you live and earn fees as a ghost:

• Before you say no to any ghostwriting project, run it through the money test. Consider how much time you'll have to put into the project . . . and what else you might be doing instead of writing for the client.

• Say yes if a project offers mediocre money but would look great on your resume and you have the time.

• Write every day, whether it's your work or a client's. If you take your own work seriously others will, too.

• If you have trouble starting on the ghosted work each day, reread the last five pages of what you've previously written. Write at least ten keepers (good pages) a day. Get through a draft, then worry later about making every word perfect.

• Get organized. If you're not, learn how. Have all your supplies close at hand. Make telephone calls at a specific time in the day and use your answering machine to screen unwanted calls. Become time conscious. Delegate, hire, or eliminate.

• Designate one room for your office. Moving your client's manuscript from the dining room table to serve food makes your work seem less essential. What do you need to make a home office work? A door that shuts. You need a quiet place in which you can create, a typewriter or computer system, reference books, a telephone, a chair. Make your office inviting and you'll want to work.

• Gear your work hours to your body clock.

• Give every single project 100 percent of your professionalism and enthusiasm . . . even with noncreative efforts. Make sure you're proud of each endeavor because even if your name isn't on it, your professional reputation is on the line.

• Read as if your job depends on it . . . it could. Most ghosts pour over newspapers and magazines, especially the popular ones. Newsmakers fill these pages and these people need the services of ghostwriters.

• Think, dress, and act like a businessperson. The competition is stiff; the best writers get the best clients.

• When your office is in your home, you'll be called or visited by well-meaning friends. Gently let those you love understand that you work regular office hours, have commitments to clients (and yourself), and have work that must be completed. It's your job; it's not a hobby.

• Don't be afraid to take a few days off. If you were working in an office, you'd have at least one day of rest. Relax your mind and do something totally removed from writing. Although you don't get a paid vacation, take a trip or pack a lunch and go to the park or the zoo. Thoughts you were previously struggling over could suddenly gel by resting your brain cells.

• If you're not involved in a fitness program and you rarely eat a healthy meal, don't expect to feel or write your best. You are the product; keep that product in shape.

• Writer's block is a hoax perpetuated by unsuccessful writers. For information on coping with and eliminating writer's block, see chapter 7.

• Be true to yourself and examine your strong points. If you are an expert in one area, one category, stick with it. If you love to write and can cook, consider ghosting a cookbook. If you work with the disabled, propose to ghost a school district superintendent's newsletter for parents of the handicapped. In short create your own opportunities to fit your personality as a writer.

• Update your resume often. It's an ego boost for any ghost to add more credits to his or her resume. Always have a copy available.

• Ghostwriting and pleasure rarely mix. You'll have a confidential relationship with your boss, but you two do not necessarily have to become bosom buddies. Your craft requires you to bill a client. Would you charge friends?

4.8   What Is Reimbursable

Always consult your accountant for specific questions on what is deductible, but here are a few general rules.

You'll need a simple bookkeeping system consisting of a journal to record your project's client, subject, date, and fee and, if it's a partial payment, the outstanding balance. (I always photocopy clients' checks, attaching the copy to my invoice, then making a notation in my account book and filing both pieces of paper. The copy provides a permanent record.)

Keep another accounting journal to record your expenses. Write checks. Attach a note to the receipt with the purchase/service. When writing a check for a work-related expense, write a note on the memo line.

Stationery stores have bookkeeping journals—get one

today. It's easier to keep the records up-to-date than to have to pull them together at the end of the year.

Keep a daily calendar of where you go, whom you see, where you eat if you're out on business, how much it costs, whom you treated (including the tip), and the reason for the trip and any mileage. If you're ever audited by the IRS your calendar will substantiate your activities and records.

The stationery store will also sell telephone logs. If you're working with a number of clients, it's far easier to record all long-distance telephone calls . . . as you make them . . . than have to sort through your telephone bills. You can, of course, make your own log.

Here's a sample:

Telephone Record Log

Date	City Called	Area Code/ Number	Person Called	Client
9/3	Los Angeles	(213) 555-4355	Bob Drake	Jackson
9/4	Newport	(714) 555-9959	Kay Kool	Smith
9/4	San Fran.	(415) 555-5554	G. Conrad	Smith

What's deductible? Business-related expenses. If you take a client to lunch, if you buy a reference book, if you turn a spare bedroom into an office and buy equipment, you're covered. The IRS has information on requirements for deductions as should your accountant or tax preparer. Public libraries also carry a wealth of tax-information books and forms.

4.9 Agreements with Your Clients

You can do business on a handshake, but contracts always make sound sense. Be prepared with a sample before it is requested and you'll be considered a professional ghostwriter. Often, when working with experts, they'll depend on you, the ghost, to provide a contract or a commitment letter. Keep a standard form on computer disk or in a file, so you can discuss the points with your client and format a compatible agreement.

To be successful, you need to know something about contracts. The following are presented *to provide information only.* A literary or publishing attorney, or your agent, should be the final authority on all agreements.

Letter Of Commitment

If you've discussed your role with a client, agreed to ghost a certain project and you begin, at the very least confirm what you discussed in a letter. A literary attorney suggests having the client confirm what work is intended by signing and returning a copy of the letter.

This letter of commitment needn't be complex. Simply state what you both discussed, your role and the client's, how you'll be paid, deadlines, and if you're working as a contractor (on a work-for-hire basis), the royalties, or the hourly rate. You may want to include a parachute clause . . . how you both can get out of the agreement and what happens to the material and money, should the relationship not work out.

Letters of commitment are often used for short-term projects such as booklets, speeches, query letters, and reports.

[Sample—for information only]

Date

Client's name/address

Dear (client's name):

This letter of commitment confirms our conversation on (date) regarding my work on your (specific project). I understand that I am to (specific requirements, listing if necessary as no. 1, no. 2, no. 3, etc.).

I understand I am working as a ghostwriter (spell out work-for-hire or other agreed-to compensation method) and will be paid (payment schedule—fee, hourly, by the word, per project). I understand I will bill you (when?) and that invoices are payable (when?). I will be reimbursed for (what?).

Should either of us be unable to fulfill our commitment, we will dissolve this relationship in a highly professional manner. I will return all material and charge at the hourly rate of (rate) for partial services.

Please sign and return one copy of this letter to me if you're in agreement with the terms. Thank you and I look forward to the opportunity to work with you on this project.

Sincerely,   AGREED AND ACCEPTED

Your name   Client's Name   Date

Statement Of Intent

A statement of intent is a contract between a client and a ghostwriter. It is a more detailed version of the letter of commitment and it's just as valid as a collaboration or ghostwriting agreement. It is written to promote clear communication for both parties on a project. Many ghostwriters use the statement of intent format for work on book proposals, technical books, novels, and other ghosted projects.

This letter of intent is an example of a work-for-hire arrangement. It can be altered for other forms of compensation, that is, hourly rate and royalty work.

STATEMENT OF INTENT/GHOSTWRITER

This letter memorializes our intent, agreement, and thoughts for our work together on your book.

Eva Shaw, hereinafter referred to as the "ghostwriter," and _____, hereinafter referred to as "author," agree as follows:

I will work for you as a ghostwriter.

1. I am not a coauthor, meaning you will be recognized as the author of the book, unless you specifically work with other coauthors. The publisher will know that I am the ghostwriter and I will receive a byline in smaller print on the book cover acknowledging that I participated in the project.

2. I will follow your lead in the major ideas and the research, if any, for the book. I will participate in the

process in a creative and cooperative manner, contributing my writing skills, my ideas, and experience in the way which is most satisfactory to our mutual benefit.

3. As a ghostwriter on this project, I understand that the main ideas for the project, namely the context and research you have developed, and the text as outlined, are your property, and I have no interest in the project except as specified in this contract. I will not write books or articles using these ideas or research that might compete with your book for a period of two years. Further I will keep all pertinent details of our project and manuscript confidential until you direct me to release the information.

4. I will work on this book as an independent contractor at a flat rate of $_____ except as noted in paragraphs _____, _____, and _____ below.

5. I understand that signing this agreement will commit us, insofar as possible, to the completion of this project, unless we mutually agree to dissolve our agreement.

6. Neither party shall be deemed at fault if either performance or the obligations required by this agreement are delayed or become impossible because of any act of God or earthquake, fire, strike, sickness, accident, civil commotion, epidemic, act of government, agencies or officers, or any other legitimate cause beyond the control of the parties. Upon the occurrence of any such event, or if the ghostwriter fails to perform any or all of the conditions or covenants of this agreement because of circumstances beyond the control of the ghostwriter and not induced or brought about by the unreasonable acts of the actual writer, at either party election, they may give notice to extend the terms of this agreement or may abandon the project altogether.

7. The services of both the author and ghostwriter to be performed under this agreement are special, unique, unusual, extraordinary, and of an intellectual character that gives the mutual services a particular value, the loss of which cannot reasonably or adequately be compensated in damages or at an action at law; therefore, the parties to this agreement stipulate and agree that, in addition to all other rights and remedies under this agreement and the law, either party shall be entitled to an injunction or other equitable remedies to prevent a breach of this contract.

8. Ghostwriter is to receive $_____ at the signing of this agreement as an advance on the project and $_____ when the author receives the first draft. Invoices will be sent and are payable upon receipt. Should the author, coauthors, publisher and/or agents thereof require extensive changes in the project after the author has accepted it, all further work will be done at a flat hourly rate of $_____ per hour. Ghostwriter is to be reimbursed for all out-of-pocket expenses and costs. Expenses and costs include, but are not limited to, telephone calls, postage, facsimile expenses, photocopying charges, research material, and travel expenses. Invoices will be sent on a monthly basis and are payable upon receipt.

9. Should extensive discussions and meetings be required with other coauthors, agents and/or publishers, and the ghostwriter's presence is desired, the ghostwriter will bill at a flat hourly rate of $_____ per hour for all such meetings plus costs.

10. Ghostwriter will make every reasonable effort to complete this book project within six months of the signing of this agreement. Author to inform ghostwriter

at the execution of this agreement as to the format of the completed project, that is, IBM compatible computer disk, WordPerfect 5.0, or hard copy typed on bond paper.

11. Ghostwriter will provide author with referrals to publishers and/or literary agents to place the project and will provide professional support as a benefit of ghostwriter's experience in the publishing and distribution aspect of this book.

12. If this book should sell over 100,000 copies, ghostwriter will receive a bonus of $5,000 in addition to the above contracted amount. If this book sells over 300,000 copies, the ghostwriter will receive the sum of $10,000 in addition to the above contracted amount. If the book sells over 1 million copies, ghostwriter will receive an additional $30,000 above the contracted amount. Should this book become adapted for television, screenplay, video, or some other electronic means of publication or communication, the ghostwriter shall be entitled to 30 percent of the royalties due the author. The author's name will appear on the copyright of the adapted script or screenplay, with the ghostwriter's name appearing in smaller type. The terms and conditions of this contract will be incorporated in a rider on the book contract that you will receive from the publisher and payment will be made to me through your publisher, agent, or producer.

13. The rights under this agreement/contract are survivable, meaning that if the author or ghostwriter should die, the respective rights can be transferred to their estates.

14. Author hereby gives ghostwriter a secured interest in this book.

15. If any portion or part of this contract is determined to be invalid, the balance of the contract will remain in full force and effect and the portion deemed to have no force and effect will be severed from the contract.

16. Should either the author or the ghostwriter fail to cooperate with one another or the parties reach an impasse, any and all disputes should be resolved through (binding) arbitration. Said arbitration can be done through community mediation, or judicial arbitration and mediation services. It is the intent of this clause to avoid the time, trouble, hazards, delays, and expenses of litigation over doubtful and disputed claims.

17. The prevailing party at the arbitration will be entitled to attorney fees.

18. Should any dispute arise under this contract, the parties herein agree that the laws of the State of _____ apply to this contract. If a dispute should arise, either party may serve the other by certified mail a notice or request for arbitration. The arbitration must occur within ninety days of such notice.

19. This contract includes all agreements between parties and any subsequent modification to this contract must be in writing, signed by both parties within one month from the date of my signature.

20. We understand that this is a legal contract and that it does not replace the personal trust and good faith established by our actions.

Dated:_____

_____
Eva Klein Shaw
Ghostwriter

Dated:_____

_____
Author

A *Writing Partnership Agreement*

The following collaboration-partnership agreement is more formal. It is, of course, meant as an example. This agreement is for a book that has been contracted with a publisher and the client (the "Author") arranges to hire a ghost. It is used on a book project of substance and may be provided by your literary agent. (Collaboration agreement is courtesy of literary agent Bert Holtje, of James Peter Associates.)

[Sample—for information only]

Agreement made as of (insert date) by and between _____ (hereinafter called Author 1) and _____ (hereinafter called Author 2):

WHEREAS, the parties desire to collaborate on a project tentatively titled _____ (hereinafter called the Work).

NOW, THEREFORE, in consideration of the premised and of the mutual promises and undertakings herein contained, and for other good and valuable consideration, the receipt of which is hereby acknowledged, the parties agree as follows:

1. The parties agree to make themselves available to each other at times and places mutually agreeable to discuss the Work.

2. The parties agree that the primary responsibilities of Author 1 with respect to the Work shall be to research and write the rough draft, and the primary responsibilities of Author 2 with respect to the work shall be to edit, revise, and when necessary to rewrite the work.

3. The parties will use their best efforts to complete a manuscript satisfactory to both parties, and to the publisher, ready for submission as stated in the Publisher's Agreement.

4. The parties contemplate the complete manuscript will be approximately _____ words/pages in length and contain _____ illustrations, if appropriate.

5. The parties intend that their contributions to the Work be merged into inseparable or interdependent parts of a unitary whole, so that the Work shall be a joint work.

6. The Work shall be the copyright of Author 1.

7. Author 1 and Author 2 shall receive equal credit as authors. Author 1 shall appear first wherever the names of the authors are printed on the Work.

8. All expenses necessary in preparation of the Work and to the negotiation of contracts for exploitation of the Work shall be the responsibility of Author 1.

9. All income from any exploitation of the Work including, but not limited to, any contract with a publisher, shall be divided as follows: Author 1, 50 percent, Author 2, 50 percent. All contracts relating to exploitation of the Work shall provide for royalty payments in the proportions stated in this paragraph.

10. Authors hereby appoint (agent's name) to receive all monies payable to Authors from Publisher as full and valid discharge of their obligations under this agreement. Agent is fully authorized to act on behalf of Authors in all matters arising out of or under this agreement. For services rendered to Authors, Agent is hereby authorized to receive 15 percent of all monies due Authors under this agreement, with the exception of direct expenses paid to Authors by the Publisher as might be required for the production of the Work. Agent hereby

agrees to remit all monies due to Authors, less Agent's commission, within ten working days of receipt from Publisher accompanied by Agent's statement and a copy of Publisher's statement.

11. If at any time the parties cannot agree on editorial matters relating to the Work, the parties will attempt to negotiate such differences. If they cannot resolve such differences after thirty days, either party may terminate this agreement by written notice to the other and reconciliation of any expenses, or the parties shall appoint a mutually acceptable third party to arbitrate such editorial dispute and the parties shall agree to abide promptly by the determination of the arbitrator. In the event of such termination, neither party will make any use of the material prepared in connection with the Work without the written consent of the other. Should termination of this agreement result in cancellation of any contract pursuant to which any advance was paid, each party shall be responsible for repayment of his or her share of such advance. Should such termination of this agreement result in breach of contract with a publisher or other licensee of the Work, and suit is instituted for such breach, the parties shall share the cost of defense for any damages awarded according to income division stated in Paragraph 9.

12. In the event of default by either or both Authors according to the terms of any third-party agreement, any monies advanced by said third parties including, but not limited to, grants, advances against royalties, or payment of manuscript preparation expenses are the sole and full responsibilities of the Authors and Authors hold Agent harmless for demands for the return or reimbursement of any portion of such funds by said third party.

13. The parties agree to share the Author's responsibility of warranty and indemnity as expressed in any contract for the exploitation of the Work, including reasonable attorney's fees, except in any instance where any breach is the result of negligence of one of the parties (including, but not limited to, failure to obtain permissions or other unauthorized use of copyrighted material), then such party will be solely responsible for any costs or damages incurred by the Publisher or any licensee of the Work and by the nonresponsible party.

14. The parties agree neither will incorporate material based on or derived from the Work in any subsequent work without the consent of the other.

15. Any controversy or claim arising out of or relating to this agreement or any breach thereof shall be settled by arbitration in accordance with the rules of the American Arbitration Association and any award rendered by said arbitrators shall be treated as a final and nonappealable judgment of any court having jurisdiction thereof. The preceding sentence shall not apply to disputes concerning the editorial content of the Work.

16. If either party should die, become incapacitated, or for any other reason reasonably beyond his or her control be unable to complete such party's responsibilities with respect to the Work prior to completion of the Work (the Nonparticipating Party), the other party (the Participating Party) may either:

(a) complete the Work (both text and illustrations) him- or herself, in which case the Nonparticipating Party's share of the income accruing from the exploitation of the Work shall be proportionate to the amount of the Nonparticipating Party's written contribution to the completed Work, or

(b) retain a third party or parties to complete the Work (both text and illustrations), in which case the reasonable compensation to such third party or parties for completing the Work shall be deducted from the Nonparticipating Party's share of the income accruing from the exploitation of the Work, provided that the Participating Party shall determine what copyright interest, if any, said third party or parties shall receive.

In either case, the Participating Party may make changes in and edit materials previously prepared; the Participating Party may alone negotiate and contract for publication and other exploitation of the Work and generally act with regard to the Work as though the Participating Party were the sole author, and the Participating Party shall furnish the Nonparticipating Party (or that Party's estate) with a copy of the contract relating to the Work so entered into by the Participating Party.

17. If after completion of the Work, either party dies, the survivor shall have the right alone to negotiate and contract for the publication and other exploitation of the Work; make revisions in any subsequent editions and generally act with regard thereto as if he or she were the sole author, except that the remaining party shall cause the deceased party's share of the proceeds as provided hereunder to be paid to his or her or their estate, as the case may be and shall furnish to his or her or their estate copies of all contracts made by the surviving party pertaining to the Work.

18. This agreement, unless otherwise terminated under the terms hereof, shall continue for the life of any copyright in the Work.

19. This agreement shall endure to the benefit of, and shall be binding upon, the executors, administrators, heirs, and assigns of the parties.

20. This agreement constitutes the entire understanding of the parties, may be amended or modified only in writing by the parties, and shall be governed by the laws of the State of _____.

In witness whereof, the parties hereunto have set their respective hands as of the day and year first above written.

Author 1	Date
Witness of Author 1	Date
Author 2	Date
Witness of Author 2	Date

4.10   If You're Fired: Five Tips to Overcome Even *That*.

Okay, let's pretend it didn't work out. You may or may not have seen it coming and the reasons really don't matter, but now your client has hired another ghost or decided to complete the project alone. Here's what you need to know about being fired:

1. Don't pout; it's bad for your image and your business. You are allowed some time for self-examination because you don't want it to happen again.

69

2. Do get out of bed and proceed with work, continue to promote yourself as a ghost, continue to be enthusiastic. Take some risks and contact potential clients.

3. Don't spread nasty rumors about your client, regardless of how tempting. It's totally unprofessional and can actually come back to hurt you.

4. Write your former client a congratulations letter when the work is published. Don't tell every person you meet or do business with, "I'll never work with that #!*% person again." The publishing world is tiny.

5. Carry on. Write. Take a workshop. Join a writer's union or organization (see Appendix C). Continue to work at your craft and you will succeed. Let one failure get you down, and you'll never make it. Period.

CHAPTER
5

*Your Rights and Responsibilities
as a Ghostwriter*

5.1 Copyrights

Every ghost needs a working knowledge of copyrights. Partly they are your protection so you'll be paid for your work.

Copyrights vary with regard to the agreement with your client. Unless your client is a seasoned, published, expert/author, he or she will definitely have questions on the copyright laws. It might pay to write or contact the copyright office for information. Copyrights protect the originator of material against having the work stolen, plagiarized, or used without permission.

For specific information on copyrights contact: Copyright Office, Library of Congress, Washington D.C., for a free kit. The office only provides information so if you need a legal opinion, you'll have to contact a copyright attorney. A literary attorney, agent, or writers' organization representative may also help you.

Under a law effective January 1, 1978, all your work (or your client's work, if you're performing the function in a work-for-hire capacity) is automatically copyrighted the second it hits the paper. According to the law, any work produced is instantly copyrighted, regardless if you pay the ten dollars for the copyright office to register the work.

The law recognizes you (or your client) as the creator, the work's owner with privileges of ownership; that is, you can sell, trade, publish, duplicate, reprint, distribute the work any way you see fit. The copyright protection lasts your (or your client's) lifetime.

This holds true *until* the work's copyright is transferred to another party. That simply means that when your client's book (for which you worked as a ghost without any copyrights) is sold to ABC Publishing, he or she transfers the use of the material for a specific amount of money or other valuable material.

Without jeopardizing another's copyrights, under the law, you may use a small portion of someone's work without obtaining permission. This is called *fair use.* The length of material used under the fair use theory hasn't been established, but generally if you use less than five hundred words *and* credit the author, you may publish the material within your book. If you are writing an article or column, five hundred words is a lot. You must be sure that the words you use from someone else's work do not constitute a major portion and that the copy does not form your central premise.

When someone, in his or her position as an expert, discusses a topic on television that material becomes public domain. You must, of course, give the individual credit, but it's not necessary to quote a portion of the presentation or the specific name, date, and time of the broadcast.

Obviously you can't contact William Shakespeare's publisher for permission to run a quote from *Hamlet*. Such old, old material is now public domain. If registered before 1978, a copyright is good for twenty-eight years after an author's death. After 1978, it's good for fifty years after the author dies.

If you have any concerns regarding the use of another author's material, write and ask for written permission, providing specific information on how much material will be used, when it will be used, where it will be used, and in what capacity. There may be a charge for the use of the material, but it'll be nominal compared to the cost of hiring an attorney to form a defense against a charge of unlawful use of copyrighted material.

With a published work, the publisher is the one to whom the permission letter is written even though the copyright is in the author's name. Also, even with your own published material, it may be necessary to request permission for use from the publisher.

5.2 Royalties and Responsibilities

Within your contract with the client, make sure you both agree on how you'll split the royalties. The royalty is the money paid to an author each time a copy of the book is sold. Remember, an advance for a book is money paid *against* the future royalties. Only when the entire advance is paid back to the publisher through earned royalties will the author then begin to receive royalty checks.

5.3   Work-for-Hire Responsibilities

If you ghostwrite for a client and are paid a flat fee for your creative input, you hold no other rights on the work. You are working in the capacity of an independent contractor. In this instance you may want to negotiate a higher percentage of the advance or a higher fee because once the job is complete, your work is finished. You will not receive royalties.

5.4   Credit Lines: With, And, As Told To, and Without

As a ghost, you'll get credit where it's due . . . sometimes endorsing the back of a check, sometimes seeing your name (perhaps in smaller type) on the cover of the book.

"With," "and," "as told to," and "without a credit" line have fuzzy but definite distinctions in the trade. (This typically applies to books.) In magazine articles, a ghost's name normally will not appear. Before you discuss credit lines with a client, generally, here's what you need to know:

• WITH is usually (but not always) utilized with the client's name placed first on the cover in large print and then the ghostwriter's name slightly below, in smaller type. The *with* signifies that a ghost has assisted on the project (writing, slaving, sweating, etc.) but the material is that of your client. *With* is often used on how-to books, exercise books, and self-help manuals where the public realizes that the expert is just that and that the ghostwriter is the expert with words.

• AND is usually shown with both names receiving the same size type. The *and* indicates that both parties have contributed to the material. This might hold true if you are working with client, but in addition to writing, you've acted as a researcher.

• AS TOLD TO signifies that the ghost has transcribed the client's story or material to present to the reader. Autobiographies, newsy newspaper and magazine stories ("I survived one thousand days on a raft in Lake Superior"), and celebrity books usually sport the *as told to* byline. This doesn't mean, by any stretch of the imagination, that the ghost played a minor role. On the contrary those in publishing realize that without the ghost, these books would never see print.

• WITHOUT ANY CREDIT is a facet of ghostwriting every writer should know about. If you negotiate a contract and realize that you will not receive (or do not choose) credit, you will then probably want to adjust your fee accordingly. However, even if a ghost-writer's name is not on the book it doesn't negate the possibilities of referrals. People working in the publishing business know who has written what. Another alternative is for the ghost to share the copyright or to be acknowledged. The public won't pick up on this, but the publishing community will.

5.5 Responsibilities of the Ghostwriter

Here's a credo for ghostwriters . . . add more to it wherever you choose and feel free to photocopy this to place on your office wall.

1. Always do what you say and say what you'll do.
2. Enter into no contracts or relationships unless you, personally, are satisfied. There's no such thing as money for nothing.
3. Be enthusiastic about every project, every client. If you can't muster that emotion, don't accept the work.
4. Go the extra distance. Your reputation is built client by client. Few ghosts are overnight successes.
5. Take responsibility. If you've done a dynamite job, let it be known. Let others acknowledge it. If you're at fault, remedy it.

6. Finish what you start. Aim for perfection. Accept yourself and your writing as human and with flaws.
7. Do it on time . . . or before time.
8. Ask for referrals. Ask for business.
9. Make and accomplish goals.
10. Take pride in your work regardless of the pay, credit line, or material. Make it neat and complete.

CHAPTER
6

Personalities and Your Skills

6.1   Working with Clients

What will be expected of you as a professional ghost-writer? That depends on your client, your personality, and the project. Basically you will be required to capture the client's voice in words and to produce excellent prose at the minimum effort of the client. Realistically, you will be expected to be:

> A psychologist
> A confidant
> A sounding board
> A devil's advocate
> A taskmaster
> A psychic
> A whiz with turning out page after page of copy
> A certifiable candidate for Mensa
> A scribe
> A gofer
> A brilliant writer

When your client is faced with introducing you, you might be called a friend, a journalist, research assistant, or even a ghostwriter. Recently one of my new clients introduced me as her director of media presentations. Although I knew she preferred to keep my identity a secret, it was interesting to see how she skirted the fact that I somehow participated in the writing of those internationally known health columns.

The good news is that while you may play a number of roles as a ghost, if you're totally aboveboard with your client, your job will be to write. You can fix lunch if you want . . . but be forewarned, professionalism counts. Keep it businesslike, and you'll continue to make money as a ghostwriter.

How can you keep everything completely business oriented? Simple. Make appointments, be on time, come prepared. Speak in a businesslike way about work matters. You are in a working situation, not a personal one. If you play it like business, that's what it will be.

Dress like a professional, talk like a professional and your client will respect your attitude. A professional gets the job done. A friend could work on a book for a half century without completion . . . it's happened.

Part of the excitement and challenge as a ghostwriter is knowing from the start that every client is different. Just because you've worked with a doctor, don't expect the next physician to be a duplicate. It could be a whole different ball game. Working with clients is a very personal situation.

What follows are client types revealed by some seasoned ghosts. All the partners have creative minds and great senses of humor. You may never meet all of these personalities, but just in case run these scenarios through your mind:

The Hoverer: He insists that you write at his office (or home office) and every twenty minutes, drops in to see how you're doing. If you've finished a major portion of the book, you must give him a copy of the material (which he may or may not read) and then demand to meet so you can go over it word by word. The best way to handle the Hoverer is to be prepared with plenty of time, discuss your work style and the ground rules before you begin, and remember you're there to do a job.

The Know-It-All: He or she is one of the types that you can depend on to look over your research closely, question where you got the material or arrived at that conclusion, and expect you to produce draft after draft, and perhaps not ever to be satisfied with the final product. Be sure he or she understands your working relationship, the specific job each of you will have on the manuscript, and that you do charge an hourly rate should you have to do more than the specified number of drafts.

The Upstart: The Upstart wants it his way and even your best ideas become his property. Life can either be extremely simple or deathly complex working with this type. How should you handle it? If it's okay with you that this client wants full control, no problem. If not, during the initial interview and meeting (when you review the project), beat it out the door, *pronto*.

The Scared Rabbit: This client is concerned with how the material will be received by her "public," students, associates, and others. She'll probably want you to sit with her as she (or you) reads the manuscript out loud. The Scared Rabbit might even agree to something on the phone or while you're working together, then the next day, tell you it's impossible and that you misunderstood. Working with a Scared Rabbit can chill even a seasoned ghost.

You can work well with the Scared Rabbit, but be prepared to back up all your facts, have answers for everything, and become assertive as long as you know you're right. You may have to take the risk of putting the relationship on the line if too much contradiction occurs.

The Copycat: Beware of this one. This is the client who has been researching his book for years . . . photocopying material from source work and writing it into his manuscript, without giving credit. It's as if the information was his alone. While he may argue he doesn't remember the exact source, you've seen the photocopied pages he took from a published book or magazine.

The Copycat is plagiarizing; this is against the copyright laws. Working with a Copycat can also have a negative impact on your career. Ask questions politely on how he got his information, if it needs to be rewritten in his words, and if there needs to be permissions obtained. If anything seems fishy, talk with your attorney/agent.

The Pseudoinnocent: The Pseudoinnocent leads you to believe that you're in charge of the project and that you know it all because you're a professional ghostwriter with experience. Then three-quarters of the way through the book, he takes over . . . totally. The Pseudoinnocent sees how easy you make writing look and decides that he doesn't need you. He's suddenly a competent writer.

Unfortunately, there's no preparation for this one . . . every ghost has worked with one. Forewarned is forearmed but don't worry; when it happens, you won't be the first. You can save yourself hassle, however, by having specific clauses in your agreement on work completed and fee required should the project be curtailed even before you begin writing. So if the Pseudoinnocent realizes one day that he's another Ernest Hemingway or Samm Sinclair Baker you'll at least recover that much out of the episode.

The Honest-to-Goodness Expert: This type, whether a philosopher, scientist, or computer genius, knows what she's talking about. Usually they're a dream to work with. The best type of Honest-to-Goodness Expert is also the Elbow Roomer (see the next category), providing you with the material needed to write the project and giving you plenty of opportunity to understand her voice and use of words. And she's a regular trouper when it comes to professionalism.

When you come in contact with this type, cultivate your relationship. Stick with the expert and your relationship will be mutually beneficial for years, with many opportunities along the way.

The Elbow Roomer: There are two sides to the Elbow Roomer, but many ghosts consider this the best of the bunch. He'll give you plenty of chances to work by yourself while staying in tune with what's going on. But that could mean you'll have to struggle to obtain enough information to make the book come together. Working with an Elbow Roomer is a challenge some ghosts prefer.

The best method of working with the Elbow Roomer is to set up regular work sessions, have a meeting agenda prepared, follow it, and work on a time-line schedule. If you sense he may become unavailable, ask to work with a trusted assistant. Most Fortune 500 executives are Elbow Roomers.

The Total Take Charger: The Total Take Charger can be a problem in that she may want to run the entire project. If that's okay, go for it. If not, set up the policies by which you'll work. There are times in a ghost's life when it's comforting to work with a Total Take Charger . . . you know exactly what you have to do and there are no two ways about it. Working with this type is very much like working on an assembly line. But when you have other creative projects in process, assembly line work can look pretty good especially when handsome checks are part of the job.

The Laissez-Faire-er: Of all the types, the Laissez-Faire-er could be your favorite *if* you're provided with all the information, including how this client writes and talks. This type wants no part of the project, trusting you

83

totally. The responsibility is great, but if you can produce a book working with a Laissez-Faire-er, you're psychic, an excellent ghost . . . or perhaps both.

6.2 Preparation for Ghostwriting a Specific Book

You've done your homework. You've researched your client and the topic so you feel confident of your position as a ghostwriter. You've also formatted and signed a statement of intent. Your next step (most likely accomplished simultaneously) is to begin preparation for ghostwriting a specific book.

Unless you're already an expert on the topic, it's past time to read everything available on the subject on which you're expected to write. Immediately go to the library and make fast friends with the reference librarians. Also make a field trip to a large bookstore and seek out books on the same topic you'll be writing about. It might be wise to build a budget into your agreement with your client if the purchase of reference material is required. Keep all your receipts, whether for the client or the IRS.

As you begin writing, you'll profit by this initial crash course education and you'll have the material available should you be required to footnote, quote, or contact authorities.

There are some ghosts who refuse to read what the competition has written for fear of duplicating or subconsciously plagiarizing it. However, by reading other books, you'll see how and where the authors fell short on information, allowing you to make yours even better or to give it a slightly different slant or marketing hook. Also check the references cited in these books. They could lead you to some otherwise little-known sources of information.

6.3   Special Notes on Preparation

Special Note 1: If you know you will require a specific library book for some time in the writing process, but the information is too much to photocopy, make a copy of the cover of the book noting the dewey decimal number. Put the copy in your working file. There's nothing more frustrating than searching the library shelves for "that little yellow book" with the obscure title and an even more obscure quote within the pages.

Special Note 2: Clearly understand your client's approach to the reader. If your client hasn't yet imagined and discussed exactly who that reader will be, talk it through. You need to know your audience.

6.4   The Art of Writing in Your Client's Voice

If you haven't done so already, start *listening, really listening* to your client. You may have to divide your thinking process in two because you'll be required to communicate while listening to the structure, tone, texture, and energy of the client's spoken words. *Duplicating the word pattern is the essence of ghostwriting.*

Make mental and written notes on how words are formed, sentences are structured, and the basic phrases and words used in conversations. Note, too, the facial and hand gestures. These are your keys to success when writing in your client's voice.

Keep this information in your client's file. Be as specific as possible because you'll be expected to ghostwrite so that everyone (who needs to) believes your client created the completed project.

Every client has a unique voice and word pattern. Sometimes you'll use this material as is and other times, for example with a research book, it could be to your client's advantage to remove those less-than-academic phrases from the final edition.

Begin by picking up specific phrases, such as "Well, darling, that's simply divine," so that your client (a wealthy Beverly Hills matron and former movie star of the thirties) comes alive to the reader. Just make sure you've composed the written work in a style that appeals to your client.

If your client, for example a teenage rock star, uses four-letter words, you may also have to become a master with euphemisms. You can't have the rocker saying darn all the time, but he very well could lose popular appeal if his true vocabulary comes to public attention.

Clients talk about soft markets, bottom line, team play, cosmic consciousness, and billions of other key terms. Some use long, complex sentences interspersed with statistics; others prefer short, snappy, slightly whimsical phrases. Whatever, practice writing in your client's voice style until you feel comfortable enough to share a part of the work. And unless you want to, don't tell your client you're practicing with the material you're sharing. If you've done this ghostwriting job well, the client will read the material and comment on the content, not the word patterns. Or the client will smile, and ask how you can produce words that he would if he had your magnificent talent.

An exercise you may want to try, as you begin in the field of ghostwriting, is to select a character on a television show and write a short piece in his or her voice. Then repeat the exercise writing for a historical figure or a former film star. No, the articles won't be perfect and you'll probably not want to share them at a party, but you will begin to get an ear for how people say words. What's more, you'll practice how words are strung together to make speech patterns unique.

6.5   The Ethics of Ghostwriting

Throughout the book, we've talked about the topic of ethics. The truth is that sometime during your career as a ghost, you may be called on to do something illegal, immoral, personally distasteful, or a combination thereof.

As a ghost, you are the observer, the scribe, the translator for the information your client wants to present.

Unless you've entered into a partnership agreement, your professional literary opinion will be considered, but your personal opinion will not. You, personally, may not believe something is proper but your role is not that of a judge.

It does sound cold and hard but it pays to give the topic of ethics thought before you jump into or out of any relationship. There's an unwritten law of ghostwriting that states:

IF YOU TURN DOWN A PROJECT BECAUSE OF AN ETHICS ISSUE, A BETTER PROJECT WILL BE PRESENTED TO FILL THAT VOID. IF YOU TAKE IT JUST FOR THE MONEY, YOU'LL BE IN DEEP TROUBLE FAST.

Part III

THE
MECHANICS
OF
GHOSTWRITING

CHAPTER
7

Before Writing the Book

7.1   The Ghostwriting Process

The process for ghostwriting a book, book proposal, magazine article, speech, or brochure can be broken down into steps. They are:

1. The client contacts you and you respond by forwarding samples of your work, your resume, and references.
2. You meet, review the project, and work out the details of the arrangement. Money, as discussed before, is a pertinent issue and so you discuss the proposed budget. The consensus among ghosts is that if you do not know the client it's wise to obtain at least half of the fee before work is begun on short projects. On longer projects (novels, nonfiction, etc.) the payment schedule must be called out in your contract. Again, you'll want some of the money "up front."

   At this time you might contact the client's editor

or agent to make sure you know all the details of the project. You must clarify this aspect in the beginning of the job because, as discussed previously, your presence might not be known to others and your client may just want to keep it that way.

3. You return to your office and write the material.
4. You give a draft of the material to the client.
5. He or she reviews the draft, makes comments (suggestions/changes/you-name-it), and you go back to work.
6. You rewrite or enhance the material and present your client with the final draft or present it to the editor, depending on your responsibility to the client.
7. You're paid the final amount, and you keep the client as a reference or a regular account.

Every single client, every single project on which you work will be distinctive . . . that's the only constant in ghostwriting.

It's the challenge, the thrill, the surge of adrenaline, the thought of living on the edge of creativity that makes a ghostwriter's life enticing.

7.2   Setting Up a Time Line

Set a schedule. Whether you share this information with your client is a personal decision. Not every ghost sets up a time line or makes a specific deadline, but the ones who are professional do. You may want to make up two time lines, one in which you include specific notes and the other to give to the client so you both know what to expect per the schedule as the project progresses.

Why make a time line when part of the pleasure of being a ghost is working at your own personal schedule? It's far too easy to allow other emergencies to slip in. The old saying of being too busy fighting off the alligators to drain the swamp is appropriate for those ghosts who work with a number of clients. Long-term projects (say writing a lengthy book) can easily and dangerously slip to the back burner. The quickies pay, but if you're committed to doing that book and it's not written, you'll lose your credibility.

Here's a sample time line used on a recent book about home-based businesses:

Book Title and Client's name

First payment:	February 1, $5,500
Start date:	February 1, mtg. 8:30 A.M., Ms. T's office
Meetings:	Every Monday, Ms. T's office, 8:30
Outline of book:	March 1 (one month after start date)
Second payment:	Invoiced, per agreement
First draft:	May 1 (two months after approval of outline by the client)
Third payment:	Invoiced, per agreement
Second draft:	Final draft, July 1 (four months after approval of outline by client)
Fourth payment:	July 1
Submitted to Publisher:	After approval by client

Depending on your work style and your client, you may need to work with a more comprehensive time line. Here are items to insert:

1. When research will be completed.
2. Times, dates, and places for work sessions with client.
3. Times, dates, and specific information for interviews with participants in the project.
4. Drafts or chapters submitted to publisher/agent.

You may want to format a master time line to input more information such as other clients' projects, assignments from magazines, your teaching/speaking engagements. You can keep all this information on a desk calendar, but having it on your computer or in a printed time line puts your deadlines in a more visual context.

7.3 Getting Ready to Write

Designate one file cabinet, a file box, or spot on your desk (or floor) or bookshelf for each book or client. I use large, plastic stackable storage bins. Organize files for the drafts, research material, research-in-process, extra material, interviews, resources, and miscellaneous. How intricate you make the filing system depends on you.

Be sure to designate one computer disk for each client and that client's specific (current) project. If your computer doesn't automatically store data at set intervals, do so after completing a certain number of pages. Make it a habit. Power does fail, problems happen, your pet iguana steps on your electrical cord and the words disappear from the screen. At the end of each work session, make a duplicate from the hard disk or a duplicate working disk. Trust this recommendation and you'll sleep better.

7.4 Verifying Facts and Gathering Information

At this point you should be extremely clear about the course your ghosted project will take. You may not be quite in control of all the facets on the book, as you will be when the outline is complete, but you understand overall how to get from Point A (the idea) to Point Z (the completed book).

This is the time to communicate clearly with your client and brainstorm about various angles, saleable information, contacts, and verification of facts. If you are writing a book about your client sledding across the Yukon, you must know *exactly* when that time was so that you can pull in other historical information. If the client plans to mention individuals who have a public image, you must begin to verify that a contact is there.

This is not the time to be shy. If you require precise facts and information, you must convey your need to your client. If you require time with the client's family, friends, or associates, ask. If you require information from individuals who expect payment in return for the information, let your client know that too.

Many ghosts write a list of the information they need, with a date that it must be returned so that the work can begin. Your client can write out the information, tape it, and send you the tape or call you with the facts. As long as you're both working from the same list, you can quickly input the facts and then get on with the outline.

While discussing the outline of the book with your client, it's time to ask for all appropriate additional background information. This may be a series of books that had a great impact on him or her, people known to the client, books that are out of print but you must locate, family diaries, and in the case of nonfiction self-help work, research books that will provide you with the background to be able to write as if your client was doing the writing.

Gathering information about your project will give you more than enough material to start the research process. You can always condense the material—but it's tough to flesh out meager facts.

7.5   Outlining the Book: The Blitz, Bubble, and Traditional Methods

An outline of a book, magazine article, report, or brochure is a condensed version by topic, listed in sequence. Before you cringe at the word outline, vividly remembering high-school English classes and those dreadful assignments, here are methods that work well to get both you and your client started: the blitz list, the bubble method, and a review of the good old-fashioned outline.

Depending on your client, after you have the chapter outline, it's time to discuss it in detail. The outline is the master plan, so it's essential that there's agreement on the information to be included.

The Blitz Method: This is brainstorming at its finest. You may want to do the Blitz or both you and your client can do it alone, then consolidate. Write down every possible, even remotely conceivable, thing you could ever, in your entire life, want to include in this book. Don't worry that it sounds inane, ludicrous, and/or preposterous. Some of the very best ideas happen this way. Do not try to write them in any order . . . you'll do that with the next step.

Once you have a Blitz list complete, let it sit overnight, then add more if necessary before putting the topics together in some type of sequence—major events, years, information needed to substantiate your conclusion. You may have leftovers—not to worry—just list those at the end.

While you're putting the Blitz list in order, you'll probably include more details. Allow plenty of room to write between the lines. Many find it beneficial to triple-space this outline.

From this list, and knowing that you must move from the concept to the completed book, organize another list on a fresh sheet of paper. This is the rough outline. It's recommended that the client participate in this if he or she works closely with you.

(If you have a potential client who wants to hire you to write a book, but he or she or you doesn't know if there's enough material, suggest the Blitz list method. Charge your hourly fee for participation. The Blitz method is an excellent test because if there's not enough material, it's far better to know it before you begin than halfway through the book—for both your sakes.)

The Bubble Method: In the center of a large piece of paper (some people use poster board or a giant sheet of newsprint) write the topic of the book and circle it. Next concentrate on its ten-to-twenty main points. Write each idea down, again circling it, and draw a line into the main bubble leaving enough room in the individual bubbles to add a number. These, then, are your chapters.

After you've decided on the number of chapters (the individual bubbles), start with a new piece of paper, placing the chapter topics (the individual bubbles) in the center and repeat as above. Continue to bubble until you're completely satisfied with most of the material.

The Traditional, Good Old-Fashioned Outline: For those with an extremely logical mind, the methods above might be too loose. If so, revert to the Roman numeral format you learned in school. But before you get bogged down in what you'll write, consider using the methods above to gain a broad, fresh perspective on your topic.

7.6   The Detailed Chapter Outline

This is your master plan, your recipe for success. You will definitely vary from the original outline, but regardless of the genre, an outline assures that you will cover everything in a sequence. There are some manuscripts that are written strictly from the client's brain, but remember, while you might be intuitive, you may not know exactly what your client wants in his or her book without the outline. Make it as detailed as you find necessary.

If you're new to ghostwriting, you will feel far more competent if you itemize. If you've known a client for a while, you may be able to work from vast concepts, rather than specific facts. Have your outline approved before you begin . . . initialed by your client if there are any concerns.

Here are a few detailed chapters excerpted from a project, a book on running for people over fifty, ghosted for a well-known sports physiologist. Initially the Blitz list method was used.

FOREWORD
INTRODUCTION
CHAPTER 1: *The More for Less Theory.* Explanation of the Masters Running Program. Why walk when you can run? This is a how-to book, the four-phase MRP. A pep-talk chapter to get the master runner primed to participate in the MRP. Quotes and statistics along with

testimonials from runners round out the chapter. Format of the program and the book are discussed here.

A question-and-answer format with annotation of the page on which to locate the material is included at the end of each chapter.

CHAPTER 2: *Running for a Lifetime.* Includes self-testing for fitness and life-style, and medical tests that are recommended after test evaluation and what the results of the tests mean, such as the comprehensive blood-testing SMAK 24. Also in this chapter are discussions on: fitness and the true meaning of aerobic; body composition and somatotyping; the physiological effect of running for the master runner; comparison of running to other fitness activities; type of person who succeeds on a fitness program and why (with a quiz offered for motivation); requirements for an effective fitness program with the guidelines of the American College of Sports Medicine.

Chapter 2 also includes goals and objectives on making running a habit, with twenty tips on achieving a healthier body and mind through running. It concludes with how the techniques that competitive athletes have used throughout the years can be applied to the goals of master runners who want to achieve a higher level of health.

Chapters 3 through 10 continue with the same technicalities, in as specific detail as was needed for the concept of the book. This book had chapter titles—some books don't.

A few words on titles: Make them memorable, but not precious. A book with a great name can make a difference in that it will have instant appeal, although a poor title will not hinder a fine book.

The detailed chapter outline should include particulars that are required in that chapter—statistics, cartoons, anecdotes, photos, and graphs.

While writing the book, keep your master outline close at hand. Feel free to change minor details or move information, but unless you discuss major revisions with your client (and his or her publisher), stay with the outline as agreed to. Life will be easier.

7.7   Planning the Format of the Manuscript

You and your client may be working with a specific format designed by the publisher—the design of the pages as they look once the book has been printed. You may be in charge of the format or it may have been decided when the book was in the proposal stage.

There are a number of options in formatting. If it's up to you to make a recommendation or a decision, your first step is to select some books that you find especially innovative, easy to understand, or clearly arranged to speed the access of material. The books do not necessarily have to be on your same topic, but it might help you understand what is the accepted format by reviewing competing books. Deciding on the format of the book is a simultaneous decision while the outlining is in process.

This book is written in sections, with chapters and

subchapters. Information is easy to locate because of the numbering system. Since this is a series book (one of many addressed to writers) all the books have the same organizational pattern.

Once you've located a few books with formats you think will be applicable to your project, discuss the decision with your client, publisher, or agent. Considerations along with format are:

- Sidebars—short, less than four hundred words—topics of information that can stand alone, but enhance the text of the book.
- Diagrams, such as maps, anatomical drawings, specific exercise routines.
- Questions and answers at the end of the chapters or additional reading.
- Text previews and reviews within each chapter.
- Tips, additional information, or motivational thoughts normally boxed in a thick line.
- List information bulleted or numbered to provide easy access to the facts or instructions.
- Inspirational quotes, photos, graphs, or cartoons with which to begin each chapter.

Select the format of the book and use it. It's a sign of professionalism to carry a concept completely through the manuscript . . . and since ghosts build their reputation one book at a time, it will be to your benefit to stay with the format you select after it has been approved by the client.

7.8   Requests for Permission (Releases)

Illustrations, cartoons, photos, and quotes all make a book more interesting. But in order to use this type of material, unless it is the client's original work, you must have releases and/or permission from the originator. It could be in violation of the law to use another artist's property without specific permission.

While you are hired as a ghostwriter strictly to write a client's book, you will also be playing the role of advisor. This is especially true when dealing with a first-time author who is using your service. Sure it would be the client who has broken the copyright law, but that violation will reflect directly back on you. Generally you must obtain written permission to use photos, interviews, charts, graphs, illustrations, and excerpts from any creative material.

Recently I was hired to ghostwrite a book about successful entrepreneurs, interviewing over fifty women throughout the United States. Before any of the interviews or photos appeared in the book, a photo and interview release were signed and returned to the client's office. This might seem like an unnecessary task (that's what the client questioned), but unless the individuals knew before participating that they were not to be paid for the use of the photo or their business advice, the subjects could come back to the client expecting their share of the profits when the book was published.

For information only here's a sample release. You may

want to contact your agent, publisher, or literary attorney for a more comprehensive one, but this release can be used for a number of purposes.

Client's Name/Address　　　　　Date

INTERVIEW AND PHOTO RELEASE

I, _____ (interviewee's name), give my permission to (your client/your name) to use my interview and photograph in conjunction with the new book _____ (add working title of book).

I understand that no payment is expected for the use of the interview or photo. I do ___/I do not ___ (choose one) wish to be given the opportunity to review the interview before the book is published.

_____　　　　_____
Signature　　　　　　　　Date

The client may be asked to pay permission or use fees. This should be the responsibility of your client (and most likely not covered or reimbursable by the publishing contract). Discuss this with him or her and your responsibilities for obtaining the releases.

Keep in mind that not everyone feels the project is as important as you do, so give participants plenty of time. Most ghostwriters request permissions and schedule interviews at the onset of the writing process. Should someone refuse to give a release of the material, the ghost must discuss that fact with the client and look at options.

7.9 Working with Artists, Photographers, Proofreaders, and Indexers

Don't be surprised if you're asked to play a key role in assisting your client in securing other creative staff for the book project. Make sure you are being adequately reimbursed for your time—or you could become a secretary and not a ghostwriter.

Gather information and *present options.* Do not—ever—make a decision without consulting your client unless you have specific authority to do so. This is his or her book and unless you have permission you could commit a major faux pas.

How do you locate an illustrator, indexer, or freelance proofreader? Network with other writers in your area, check the yellow pages, or contact a publisher to ascertain who did the illustrations in a book your client has admired to find the right person for this new project.

It pays to do some comparative shopping, and your client may want to hire the individual to do a small sample of work to see his or her expertise. Ask for other examples of the individual's work, check references, and then rely on your intuition. Your client may ask for your advice so be ready with a logical opinion.

People will share the intimate details of their personal lives, but when it comes to money, they often feel violated. Your client may not feel comfortable having you review his or her contract with a publisher. However, as the ghost, you must know if there is money built into the agreement to hire additional support.

Normally it is up to the author (your client) to pay for drawings, photos, use permission, and photo permission out of the advance. Ask your client what he has budgeted for an artist, indexing assistant, or photographer.

In the most professional manner inform the client that he or she must be ready to pay professional wages for professional work. Cutting corners on this aspect can undermine other facets of the project. You'll want to familiarize yourself with the cost of these services in your area prior to needing them.

Before you attempt to locate the right person for the project, you must be extremely clear on what you require. You and your client may want to write an outline or short summary of the specific details. Here's an example of illustration requirements for a book on canine training:

Each illustration will be presented on an eight-by-ten-inch poster board, camera-ready, for the breed depicted in the photograph. For information on the poses in each drawing, the artist will work from photos of the author and her dog. All work is to be completed by (date) and all work is to be done on a work-for-hire basis. No copyrights will be retained by the artist. The assignment includes:

• Ten (10) pen-and-ink drawings of a woman training her medium-size dog to sit using the ten-step program.

- Ten (10) pen-and-ink drawings of a child teaching his dog various tricks.
- Two (2) pen-and-ink drawings of a couple briskly walking their dog showing the difference between walking with a small breed and a large breed.

The artist, illustrator, photographer, or other creative individual may refuse to sell all copyrights, but this is a negotiable point with the client and the artist. Be specific on the rights your client is buying and whether or not the individual will expect credit in the book.

7.10   How to Deal with Writer's Block

Writer's block is a joke to professional ghosts. Ghostwriters are in a service industry and hardly ever await inspiration. It's ludicrous to think of your dentist, dry cleaner, or the individual who operates the camera store around the corner waiting until the mood strikes to attend a customer.

There are no bolts of lightning or messages from beyond on how to construct an articulate sentence or keep a reader on the edge of a chair. Don't allow the misconception that writers are different and thus permitted to have creative barricades strangle you as you progress in this field.

If words don't come, get out of the office for an hour, take a walk or get some exercise, then get back to work on

107

that project or another one on which you've been hired to write. If you were the employee and your alter ego was *the boss*, could you afford to have that writer sit on his or her derriere waiting for sheer creativity to manipulate the computer keys? Hardly.

If all else fails start a different writing project or another section of the same book. Sometimes first chapters are almost impossible to get right, so smart ghosts work on another segment of the project until they're content with the feeling and flow of the words, then return to write or rewrite the initial part.

If your brain seems to be in a shut-down mode, here are some remedies . . . notice they do not include excessive eating, drinking, lunching, TV watching, or any other "ing" or activity not directly related to your project and profession:

- Go to the library for research.
- Reread material you've already written to improve it.
- Write thank-you letters to previous clients.
- Contact new or prospective clients.
- Make lists of material you'll need to complete this project.
- Query publishers and magazines about your own bylined work.
- Submit your own work.
- Organize your office and material.

- Have a quick chat with another writer discussing your current problem. Get his or her input.
- Update your resume.
- Do anything that helps your writing, so that your boss doesn't know you're stumbling.

CHAPTER
8

Learning to Love Facts

8.1 Researching with Your Client

Facts are the instruments of your occupation; they make your book, article, or project tangible. Unless you research and double-check them with care, your reputation will be in jeopardy.

As a ghostwriter there will be times when you will be responsible for the research. On other projects you'll be handed a carton of information that the client has accumulated and organized. There are scores of books on how to research. Let's concentrate here on sharing the task. With your client:

- Discuss specific techniques you both will use to research. Provide insight where you can.
- Ask questions if you don't understand.
- Make a clear plan of who will research what.
- Schedule meetings to review the research material.

One client/ghost team spends the week collecting books, magazine articles, clippings, and reports. They then meet and review every scrap of material. At that point, the information is turned over to the ghost who must organize it.

This is done to make sure all areas are included . . . not to duplicate the information that's been published.

8.2   Fact Checking

The relationship of client and ghost is built on trust. Therefore if the client provides information, you know that the facts are correct, right? Not necessarily. It pays to spot-check information, look at the original research, and review the sources yourself.

With a few months' experience you'll be able to spot a questionable statistic or quote, but when you're fresh on a project in a new area, never let a fact go by without scrutinizing it.

8.3   Finding and Hiring Help

Depending on the scope of work on a ghostwritten project, you may be expected to locate, hire, and work with research personnel. As with securing the services of illustrators and photographers discussed previously, it's most efficient to outline *exactly* what you want done.

Various writers' magazines run advertisements for individuals who offer researching services. There are also computer on-line programs that give sources for information. And on the lower end of this scale is the employment of college students who work part-time researching material for others. If you require extensive research, the third option could be a thrifty and smart move on your client's part.

Use ingenuity and your best hiring skills when securing someone to research your project . . . you do not want to have to double-check all the facts. Make it clear to the researcher that any information that is in doubt should be brought to your (or your client's) attention.

CHAPTER
9

Interviewing

9.1   The Craft of Interviewing

"Leave nothing to chance," cautions a ghost who has written for some of the top celebrities on television. Another stresses, "Keep all your notes, all your tapes." A third states, "Go by feel, then back it with brilliance."

Interviewing is an integral part of ghostwriting. You will be talking to your client when gathering information for his or her project, and listening to word structure as well as content. You'll be interviewing people who will contribute to the project. You'll also be asking questions (that's interviewing) of reference librarians, associates, and anyone else you can imagine whose opinion, assistance, or information may help the project.

How do you secure an interview? If the session is with an associate of the client, you may want the client or his/her staff member to set up the initial contact. Otherwise, it's up to you. And just how do you obtain an interview? Simple. Ask for one. Call the subject, clearly communicate why you'd like to interview him or her, ask when it would be convenient, state what you plan to ask, and make the appointment. Be prepared to:

1) make an appointment to talk with the subject so that you can arrange a time for the interview, and;

2) to do the interview at that very second. . . . It has happened and you need to be prepared.

A client may or may not want to be part of the interviewing process. Either way discuss interviewing methods with the client before you begin; he or she knows the book's topic best. If the client will be working with you on the interview process, be prepared to instruct the client on how to ask questions.

Having the client involved within each interview may be crucial if the information is of a confidential nature and/or you require the client's observations on the copy. It's helpful for the ghost to have the client involved in the interviewing process; however, for an experienced ghost, that can slow it down due to extraneous conversation.

It's up to you to know the specific information you want to secure from each of your subjects interviewed. Meet with the client before you begin, review the slant you plan to take with each interview, format questions the client believes will secure the most information, and then proceed.

Depending on your time line for the book, it makes sense to schedule all the interviews near the beginning of the project. People take business trips, change their minds or opinions, and become uncooperative among other problems, so you may have to locate substitutes if some interviewees become unavailable.

9.2   Methods of Recording Interviews

There are no right ways to interview. If it works for you, and you're able to duplicate the interview, the extract, or pertinent information when you return to your office, you've succeeded.

Try a few methods, then find the ones that work best for you. Take advantage of a number of methods throughout one project, for example:

Written interviews.   In theory, the ghost writes down every thing the subject says. In actuality, the writer would have to be a master at shorthand. Normally what really happens is that the ghost jots down pertinent phrases, long exact quotes, and recalls them when the moment to transcribe the information arises.

A problem with this method of trying to capture everything a subject says is that you are extremely busy with writing. You must continually jot down important phrases and unless you're supremely skilled, you won't be able to carry on an intelligent interview simultaneously.

In addition the subject will probably watch you, making sure that you write his or her every utterance. If you should miss something he or she believes to be consequential, he or she will probably stop you and have you go back to clarify it on your note pad. Of course this is time-consuming and can be frustrating. This interview method takes the most time and the spontaneity out of the appointment.

The key word method. In this interviewing method, the ghost writes down specific memory-jogging words, key words, or a few phrases. If there is an outstanding quote, the ghost will then transcribe it exactly. The key word method works well when doing brief interviews if certain information, facts, or statistics must be ascertained.

The tape method. Taping interviews has its plus and minus sides. The positive includes exact transcriptions, being able to hear words again and again until you can duplicate word patterns and the client's or subject's voice. You can also take your time in transcribing the interview because it will be safely stored on the tapes (placed in well-marked envelopes or boxes). The negatives include the fact that tape recorders sometimes put people off. Have you ever had a microphone stuck in your face?

Using a tape recorder successfully takes skill; the ghostwriter must warm up the subject if he or she isn't accustomed to being interviewed. This can be done by assuring the subject that you, the ghost, will quote him or her exactly and make the subject sound articulate and interesting. You can also help them be comfortable by using a micromini-sized machine. And you can assure an excellent interview by telling the subject that you didn't dare take notes because you were so delirious about meeting the person and you didn't want to be scribbling, thus possibly missing something fascinating or valuable that was said. A few ghosts simply say, "The tape recorder makes the interview much more successful."

Before the tape recorder is turned on, place it close to the subject, chat a moment or two, then hit the on switch and begin your interview. Be cognizant of time so you can turn the tape over when needed.

The memory method.   This has been nicknamed the prayer method because ghosts who don't know exactly what they're doing have to pray that it will all come back to them as they transcribe the notes. Using this method, simply interview the subject, return to the office, and at the appropriate time or part of the book project, spew forth the interview. Some ghosts do this with incredible accuracy; for most of us, it's a nightmare.

Computer method.   For those times when you're interviewing on the telephone, a timesaving device you may want to try is inputing the interview directly onto your computer. You will need to be a fast typist and be able to carry on a conversation while typing, but it can work.

Combination method.   This is the style of choice for most successful ghostwriters utilizing the written, the key word, the prayer, and the taped interview methods. Ghosts write key words, tape the interview, scribble exact quotes, and pray, at least initially, that everything will work out. The combination method gives the ghost time to listen and to jot down a phrase or the tape recorder's counter number that appears while the subject is saying something profound, and then ask the next question.

117

Even though I think this is the most professional way, as stated before, try them all and find the best way for you.

9.3   The Interview

You've secured the interview and you're ready to begin. Your client may or may not be with you . . . regardless, the system is the same. However, if you're working as a team, you should divide roles before you meet the subject.

When leaving the office, regardless of how clever you are, write out the questions. You might want to jot them down in a notebook or in the form you've created for interviews. If your client will be working with you, format your question list together. Specifically ask what information the client wants to extract from the interview.

Writing out questions prior to an interview is the sign of an experienced ghost. A professional knows that confusing situations occur and even if there is total chaos, those questions can produce a successful interview.

Telephone interviews.   Your telephone can certainly be the most efficient piece of office equipment if you routinely use it to do interviews because you'll save considerable time. Not having to drive to the interview, wait for your appointment, or even dress in a suit and tie allows you more time to produce money-making writing. You simply call beforehand to make an appointment for the call.

In order to do a competent job with a telephone interview, have your questions ready and be prepared to sound extremely interested. The subject will have to depend on your voice for encouragement.

Consult your state laws whether you must tell the subject that you are taping the interview. Always let your subject know exactly what you're doing before you turn on your equipment, and then say, "Mr. Jones, I've turned on my tape recorder now. Shall we start the interview?" After he responds, begin. It's smart, if doing a number of telephone interviews to 1) refer to your subject by name in the first few seconds since tapes can get mixed up, and, 2) keep all your tapes labeled and in a safe spot until the project is completed.

Also, before you turn your tape recorder on, you will probably want to go over the type of material you'll cover. Remember, most people, even experts, are unaccustomed to being interviewed but once you show them you are thoroughly interested in their views, they'll warm up. (More tips on questions to break the initial ice and keep the interview going occur within the next section.)

To do a taped telephone interview, you must have a tape recorder with a microphone attachment for the telephone. In addition, it's advisable to have your questions written out, and have extra paper to write down additional questions you might want to ask during the interview.

Check out the procedure before you call by dialing a friend and recording the conversation—with permission of course. One ghost discovered that whenever she taped interviews from her office telephone there was a terrible buzzing in the background when replaying the tape. She had her phone checked, replaced her tape recorder, and bought another microphone only to discover it was her new computer terminal quietly humming away . . . and being picked up by the sensitive microphone as a jack-hammer concerto.

In-person interviews. During a face-to-face interview, you must concentrate on exactly what is occurring. As with a telephone interview, be prepared with questions and write them down before you meet.

Use good posture, mirroring the body language of your subject, staying professional throughout the interview. There are times when your subject will request a copy of his or her session before it is included in the book. Make a decision with your client before you receive this request. Also have your interview release sheet ready for signature.

In addition, if at all possible, interview your subject on his or her turf. You can truly get the feel of the person when you talk with him or her in an office, home, or construction site. Yes, tape recorders are wonderful but they are excellent at picking up background noise. A little bistro may seem like a fantastic place to interview someone, but when you transcribe the tape, it could sound as if a three-ring circus was there. Certainly restaurants are difficult places to conduct interviews . . . it's advisable even if someone else is paying to choose an office, a quiet corner of a room, or the library.

Group interviews. When interviewing a group of people using a tape recorder, write down expressly how you can recognize the different voices when you transcribe the tape. For example, George might have a squeaky whine, Betty have a baritone voice, and Sam may speak in a Texas twang. No one needs to see these clues, but you'll be thankful when you get ready to incorporate the interview that you can remember who was saying what.

Translated interviews.   There may be times when you'll interview a non-English-speaking person. In this case, it's essential to watch the facial expression of the subject as you make notes or tape the conversation. While it's not necessary to speak in three-letter words, having questions ready and written down will decrease any confusion. Be sure to allow a little extra time for this type of interview and assure the translator that you will be quoting exactly from that which is translated.

9.4   An Interview Record Form

Interviewing several thousand people over the course of my career, I devised a form that can be duplicated and adapted to your personal needs. It works just as well when doing interviews with experts for a magazine article or those whom you talk with for a book. Whether you choose to use this method or not, *always* make sure you have the correct spelling of the subjects' names and know how you can reach them afterward. If you and your client are interviewing, make sure he or she has extra copies and is using the form. If you're working on a

121

book with confidential case studies and the subjects use pseudonyms, it's doubly important to obtain this information.

Don't be inhibited about spelling out even common-sounding names. For example there are a number of spellings for Linda and if you don't ask the subject, the odds are that you'll spell it incorrectly.

Interview Record/Information Sheet
Date:
Book title:
Client:
Name of interviewee:
Address/telephone:
Date/time of interview:
Release signed/photo permission obtained:
Subject of interview:
Questions/area to be covered:

Computer disk/file name:

9.5   Techniques for Great Interviews

If you and your client will be asking the questions, of course share the following information with him or her. Also add specific information for the people you'll be talking with.

- LISTEN. You are doing the interviewing. You are there to ask questions, not to join in a conversation regardless of how tempting that might be. If you can interview and still tie in a "gosh, I've always wondered . . ." type of query, go for it.

- CHECK YOUR EQUIPMENT. Prepare yourself before the interview. Write questions, make notes using key words. Check your equipment making sure the batteries in your tape recorder are fresh, your pen works, you have adequate change for the parking meter. Also confirm your appointment, if possible, and call if you think you might be late. This is an indication to your subject that you realize his or her time is valuable and you are a professional.

- EXPLAIN YOUR PURPOSE. Introduce yourself clearly and plainly. You may want to include a little small talk, the weather, season, how you traveled to the interview. This will make the subject feel more comfortable talking with you once you get down to the business at hand.

Depending on your subject, a compliment goes a long way to make you both feel more relaxed: "You have a beautiful view from this office." But don't ever, ever gush.

- ASK FOR YES AND NO. At the beginning of an interview always be aware that your subject is probably as nervous (or perhaps more so) than you. You've interviewed a lot of people, but you may be the only ghostwriter to cross the subject's path. Therefore you may want to ask a few questions that require only a yes and/ or a no answer. This allows the subject to warm up so that when you start asking tougher questions, communication has already been established.

• CHANGE THE TONE. Change the tone of the questions to keep the interest in the interview. For example, ask a simple question, then one that will require more thought. Vary the tone of your voice from strong and enthusiastic to almost a whisper.

• ASK FOR FEEL. Use questions that elicit feelings, questions that will require your subject to emotionalize the response. Be prepared, too, for the one-in-a-million subject who will only offer monosyllable answers. It is hoped you'll be a pro before you happen onto this person but, by having all your questions written down, you'll have plenty of material so you don't have to tango alone should you interview this type.

• GIVE IT A BREAK. Don't be afraid of silence, it can do wonders. Your subject is probably thinking while you're talking—most people do. When you take a breath and stop asking questions, he or she will probably fill the empty space with just the quote you've been waiting for. Eye contact and an interested facial expression let your subject know you're waiting for a response in order to continue.

In case you doubt the use of silence, remember back as a child when you did something socially unacceptable (and may have been sitting in the principal's office)? You were given "that" look and instantly came clean.

• ADD SOME SENSE. Every interview requires that you make note of the senses. Add color, smell, taste, and feel and your interview will have a larger dimension. "Do you remember what you (the client) and Greta Garbo shared at the picnic when you first met in 1932?" "What color was his shirt when (the client) and you saw Elvis perform that first time?" Bring all the senses into your interview through questions. Also make a special note of what your subject is wearing, the fragrance of perfume or after-shave, the furnishings or surroundings, the facial expressions and hand gestures. This type of information will create lively reading.

• KEEP ON TARGET. It's up to you, as the ghost-writer, to keep the interview on the topic. Make notes of anything that comes to mind in case you might forget to ask. If your subject pulls back when asked a question that's too touchy, ask another general question or three on a topic that he or she will easily be able to respond to, then rephrase the delicate question or ask it in two parts.

• WIND DOWN. Finish the interview by asking if the subject has anything to add. Ask if there are questions you didn't ask that he or she would like to answer. You'll be pleasantly surprised many times over when your subject summarizes his or her viewpoints or you get a quote that was worth all the chitchat which came before.

• LEAVE A LITTLE OF YOURSELF BEHIND. Thank your subject, shake hands, and leave your business card or your name and phone number in case you might want to add something later. And if this person is exceptionally gracious, intriguing, and/or seems to be a potential ghostwriting client for some future time, it makes shrewd business sense to follow up with a thank-you note.

9.6   Twenty Questions Guaranteed to Keep an Interview Going

Some people are naturals at being interviewed, some are bashful. You're going to encounter both types as clients and subjects in interviews. The questions that follow will not fit every interview situation, but with a little modification you can get plenty of mileage out of these ice-breaking and provocative queries. If the question piques the interest of your client or subject, if intuitively you know there's something the individual or you would like added, try, Why do you say that? or That's really intriguing, could you tell me more about . . .

1. Do you remember the first time you (and fill in the appropriate activity, such as: ate lunch in New York's Russian Tea Room)?
2. What is the greatest fallacy about you?
3. What is your most vivid childhood memory?
4. What was the toughest/easiest time of your life?

5. Growing up, what were your secret aspirations? What is the most unique profession you wanted to achieve? When did you realize that you were meant to be a (add in appropriate word)?

6. What is the biggest disillusionment you've ever experienced?

7. What do you appreciate most about yourself? What qualities do you appreciate in others (in your field, sex, religion, etc.)?

8. What do you admire least about yourself? If you could change one part of your personality (or anatomy), what would that be?

9. What are you most proud of?

10. What is the most unusual thing you've ever done?

11. What was your first impression of (your client, a natural disaster, etc.)?

12. If you had another chance, is there anything that you'd want to do differently?

13. What do people remember most about you?

14. What do you find most appealing (or annoying) about the music of this decade? (You might want to ask about government, teenagers, business, politics, or fast food according to your specific research topic.)

15. Do you believe in love at first sight? Have you ever been in love with more than one person at the same time?

16. What's the best thing about being (add profession, sex, age, or hobby)?

127

17. What is success? Are you successful?
18. Did you ever miss a chance to be really rich (famous, happy, successful, etc.)?
19. What is your favorite spot in the entire world? Why? What do you do when you're there? Describe how it looks.
20. How do you handle (add emotion or circumstance such as stress, a handicap, wealth, or poverty) in your life? (You might want to ask the same question for a profession, having ten children, or a spouse who is an astronaut.)

In respect to the specific information you must elicit, fall back on the journalist's famous six: Who, What, When, Why, Where and How. The answers will provide all the basic material for any interview.

CHAPTER
10

Selling the Idea

10.1   The Book Proposal

Writing an effective book proposal that sells a book idea is an art form in itself. Ask any author who hasn't placed his or her book if the proposal lacked spark.

Yes, a book proposal sells the book, whether the work has been written or is in the comprehensive idea format. In order to write a proposal the ghostwriter must have a complete overview of the project.

Writing a proposal requires the ghost to meet and set up a contract with the client, prepare for the writing with research and background investigation, boil down concepts, and produce a plan that sounds like ad copy with substance. The proposal must be submitted first to the client, then to the agent or publisher in a format that is most agreeable. Some ghosts feel a proposal is a stepping-stone to writing the book, and they may include a paragraph within the contract with the client that if for some reason they aren't chosen to write the book (after it's placed with a publisher) they receive remuneration.

Writing a book proposal is an exercise in communication. But make no mistake, a book proposal is a business proposal, plain and simple. It must convince the publisher, without a doubt, that money is to be made from producing a client's book.

The days of mediocre books being published are gone forever. Competition for great books is serious, but the good news is that those who establish themselves as professional ghostwriters, and can produce excellent book proposals, have as much work as they can handle.

Fiction and nonfiction proposals are specific and they must be forceful and compelling. They are not a condensed version of the book, but a proposition with a definite design, created to encourage the sale of a book to a publisher.

Once you understand the formats, writing proposals alone can become a job, even if they don't all mature into contracted ghostwriting.

Book proposals for both fiction and nonfiction are usually written before the book is. Clients who have no other publishing credits may be required to submit most of the completed book unless the ghost's name is known. And even in that case, all publishers require a proposal and at least a sample chapter of the proposed project. Writing a book proposal can be even more complicated than a book because every word must be included for a distinct reason.

Ghostwriters charge from five hundred to two thousand dollars for writing book proposals. Fees vary depending on the project and time necessary to research the proposal. Some ghosts will waive the fee for writing the proposal in exchange for a larger share of the advance. Others will charge a fee, but receive half when the work is complete and the second portion when the book advance is received. If you're asked to write a proposal, consider these options. However, unless you see the book as an absolutely sure seller, it makes better business sense to be paid on a work-for-hire basis and receive half of your fee up front and the second portion when you provide the final proposal to the client.

There will be times when a publisher or agent will be extremely interested in the proposal you've ghosted but will ask for changes. It will be up to the client to make that decision and its degree. If a publisher or agent finds the proposal so enticing that he or she has taken time to contact the client, advise your client that odds have just tripled in his or her favor. If the changes are not due to your errors, you may want to charge your client your hourly rate for the necessary alterations.

10.2   The Nonfiction Book Proposal

Like excellent advertising copy, the book proposal must stand out. Whether your client is represented by an agent or sends the proposal directly to the editor's desk, in one word the nonfiction book proposal must be: persuasive.

The proposal must persuade the publisher that he

131

would be totally mad to pass up the opportunity to publish this remarkable book. It must also persuade the editorial board and publisher's sales team that the project will make money.

After the proposal is complete, you or your client will forward it to his or her agent or to publishers. As an alternative you may want to advise your client to hire you to write query letters, outlining the finest points of your project and offering to send the proposal immediately. Query letters will save time, energy, and postage, three advantages that will appeal to a cost-conscious client. (Query letters are discussed later in this chapter.)

10.3   Format for the Nonfiction Proposal

If your client has a specific format that he or she prefers, use it. However, one that many ghosts have successfully used to sell books follows. At the end of this section is an example of a cover sheet.

1. The cover page of your proposal should be single-spaced and in a format that's clear and attractive.
2. The proposal should be double-spaced, printed on white paper with a clear type style (dot matrix isn't acceptable). Use a new printer ribbon and print on 20-pound bond paper. Continuous computer paper is okay as long as it's good quality and you've removed the feeder guides.

3. Number the pages at the bottom, putting your client's name on the top along with the title of the book, for example, Fitness Walking/Shaw. This is called the slug.

4. Never send the original (unless you're making multiple originals on your computer).

5. Send the proposal, as soon as it's ready, with a brief cover letter. Responses from publishers and agents take time—time for you to write the book for your client or work on other ghostwritten projects.

6. Neatness counts. Your proposal must be as sharp-looking as the words sound, but don't go fancy and duplicate on gray paper to be placed in a leather cover.

7. Always include a self-addressed stamped envelope with enough postage for the return of your material, if you want it back, and a letter-sized envelope or a post card if you just want a response.

8. If you want to fax the material to an agent or publisher, call and get approval first. Faxing is quick and desirable in many situations, but sometimes produces a tie-up in the facsimile machine that is meant for the publisher's business, not hopeful ghostwriters or their clients.

9. Publishers and agents vary in the time they take to respond to a query (usually less than a month) or a proposal (sometimes more than two months). Be patient, work on other assignments and projects. If you, however, don't hear about the status of your

submittal in a reasonable length of time, send a follow-up letter, wait again, then make a polite inquiry over the phone. Whether this is to be your responsibility or your client's is a point of discussion.

Here are the components of a nonfiction book proposal with explanations after the heading:

Cover page: See example that follows.

Table of contents: Do not write this page until after you've written the proposal.

Description: This is a complete overview of the entire nonfiction book. You'll want to mention who the reader will be and why the reader will buy this book. This is the sales pitch and the opportunity to discuss all finer points of the project. If it sounds like a commercial with heart and energy, you've done the job well.

How the book is different: This section gives you the opportunity to tell why this book is great. You'll want to include how the book can get more exposure than the others on the market and what makes your book even better than all the others currently available. If it happens that your proposed book will include innovative techniques or breakthroughs that have never been made public, discuss this area and what the public will gain from reading your book. Be warned: If you or your client can't figure out why your book is different (and better) than the others on the market, you don't have a marketable project.

Competition: You must provide a section within the non-fiction book proposal discussing the competition for your intended book. If you or your client haven't done so before, go directly to a major book store and review the shelves; then check other books on the competing topic in the library and *Books in Print* by subject category.

This section, "Competition," can most closely be compared to writing a mini book report, but you must also prove with each review that your book will be superior. As you format the competition part of your proposals the most accepted method is to make it look like lines on a bibliography, adding information such as price and illustrations. Continue and summarize the material in each book and why your client's will be in more demand.

Your client (and you):   This is the area within the proposal for your client to toot his or her own horn, but you'll be writing it so lay it on thick. Talk about your client's unique qualifications for writing the book, his or her background, experience, and most definitely *connections*. You may want to include academic background, media exposure, publishing credits, and, again, who your client knows.

If you're writing the book and your name will appear on the credits, you will also be expected to peddle it yourself. In all likelihood your client is depending on your writing credits to sell the project. If your name isn't to appear on the book, but your client realizes that you do have clout, you may want to include your name in brackets after the client's name. If you are to act as an invisible ghost on the project, you will, of course, leave your name completely off the proposal.

Chapter-by-chapter outline: Include at least one paragraph detailing each chapter of the intended book. Editors like the names of each chapter (if appropriate) included in the proposal. Chapter titles and the name of your book may not guarantee a sale, but provocative, catchy, or hard-hitting titles can help.

About the manuscript: Write about the format of the book and possible illustrations. If an artist has been selected, include a sample of his or her work. Address the issue of sidebars and the style in which the book will be written, that is, academic, conversational, poetic, or humorous. Discuss the length of the book. Leave nothing to chance; communicate every part of the book as you and your client visualize the final product. Editors are not mind readers.

Sample chapter: You may be asked to submit one to three sample chapters of the book. If you've already written the book, select the most compelling chapter—the finest example of your work. If the book has yet to be written, write the very best chapter you can, and at the same time make doubly sure you like what you've written because you will be compelled and contracted to continue with the book in the same format as you present.

If you have a long list of writing credits, you may be able to submit a partial chapter so that the editorial board can 1) get a feel of how you, the ghost, will produce the book, and 2) calculate the extent of editing required. This is another economic decision for the publisher so you'll want to make the book as error-free as humanly possible.

As an option: You may want to include a topic outline, the tests your client plans to conduct, the research that's anticipated or is complete. Interviews to be conducted or other pertinent information can sell your client's book to the editor and the editorial board. If your client already has someone remarkable to write an introduction or foreword, by all means shout it out and include it on the title page as well.

If your client is about to undertake an earth-shattering attempt at anything, let the editor know. Again, make all your plans known, but select your words with care, making the proposal an example of your best ghostwritten work.

(Cover sheet for nonfiction proposal)
BOOK PROPOSAL
WORKING TITLE: ##### #### ####
AUTHORS: Client's name is listed first with/and/as told to (the ghost)
FOREWORD BY: (If applicable)
CONTACT: Client's name/address/phone/fax or: Agent's contact information

10.4 Preparing a Fiction Proposal and Synopsis

Do ghostwriters write fiction? The answer is yes—as a ghost you may have the opportunity to write a novel or even specialize in the field. Review this section, store the information, and when a client approaches you with an idea for a novel, you'll be the ghost hired.

Sometimes ghostwriting a novel is considered editing, but when you ask the writer, he or she will honestly reveal that it was a total rewrite job on the client's manuscript. Sure the theme and plot remained the same, but the characters, various segments of the story, and pertinent details like location, sequence of events, and length had to be changed to make the novel marketable.

In order to ghostwrite fiction, you needn't have written saleable fiction but it helps. Thus if you're currently working on your own novel, a ghostwritten novel could be the perfect sideline. In order to ghostwrite fiction, it's essential to do your homework and read many books in the same genre as the project. For example if you are to ghostwrite a romance, start researching by reading Harlequin novels, short stories from women's magazines, and those fat, family sagas that are displayed near the checkout counter of the grocery store.

The first order of business before ghostwriting the fiction proposal and synopsis is to write to a prospective publisher or publishers and, enclosing a self-addressed stamped envelope, request a copy of their guidelines.

Study the guidelines with care; they are your map to having the material purchased. Guidelines do change; make sure the ones you're using are current.

The fiction proposal is composed of a *brief* cover letter outlining your client's qualifications for writing the book. If he or she doesn't hold writing credentials, this might include extensive travel or residence where the book takes place, academic degrees, or simply that your client is addicted to the genre. The cover letter should explain the type of novel, length, and whether it is complete, mentioning that the synopsis is enclosed, along with a self-addressed envelope.

How long should you wait for a response? That depends on how hot the book or your client is, but, generally, be patient for six weeks, then follow up with a letter asking the status of your submittal, then a phone call. Publishing is a waiting game so definitely continue working on the novel or other ghostwritten projects while the fate of one is being decided.

Writing a synopsis may be the most difficult job a ghost can tackle . . . it's not merely a condensed version of the novel, and it's not the play-by-play style of the nonfiction proposal. The synopsis, written in the present tense, should follow the guidelines below but you can alter the format depending on your topic. However, your key to selling is to refer specifically to those guidelines obtained from the publisher.

Publishers and agents know that a synopsis is difficult to write, yet the outline must dramatize the story, capture the feeling of the time period and the characters, and illustrate the tone of the novel. While writing the synopsis of the plot, keep the description down to one or two sentences and do not include lengthy characterizations. Rather, depict the essence of the main characters with the drama of the novel. The synopsis must be entertaining.

10.5   Format of the Fiction Synopsis

1. The cover page of your synopsis should be single-spaced and in a format that's clear and attractive, in the same format as the cover sheet for the nonfiction proposal. (See page 137.)
2. The synopsis should be double-spaced, printed with a clear type style (dot matrix isn't acceptable). Use a new printer ribbon and print on twenty-pound bond paper. Continuous computer paper is okay as long as it's good quality and you've removed the feeder guides.
3. Number the pages and do not exceed fifteen. Seven to ten pages is the preferred number.
4. Never send the original (unless you're making multiple originals on your computer).
5. Send the synopsis as soon as it's ready, with a brief cover letter. Responses from publishers and agents take time—time for you to write the book for your client and work on other material too.
6. Neatness counts—the synopsis must be as sharp-looking as the words sound. Don't mix romantic

notions with business, duplicating the synopsis on pink or lavender-scented paper decorated with hot pink sticky hearts. Keep it clean and as if produced by a score of secretaries.

Show how effective it will be for the publisher to buy this proposal. Yes, the story must sell the publisher, but work that is professionally prepared is truly appreciated.

7. Always include a self-addressed stamped envelope with enough postage for the return of your material, if you want it back, and a letter-sized envelope if you just want a response.

10.6   Writing Query Letters

It takes skill, intuition, and a sense of what sells to write outstanding letters. Every ghost should have a working knowledge of queries.

Queries represent you and your client. Just like the Head and Shoulders' commercial that says, "You don't get a second chance to make a first impression," if your query doesn't measure up, that's the only shot you'll get. Once a publisher or agent returns a query, it is not acceptable to send it back again. The only exception is if the publisher or agent asks for specific changes.

A query letter is written to a publisher or agent to ask if the proposal, synopsis, manuscript, article, article idea, or newspaper column concept is of interest. In addition a ghost might write a query letter to a potential client asking if the ghost's talents may be of service.

Here's a quick overview of query letters:

1. Always single-space in a traditional business style. If you're unclear of business letters, the public library has books illustrating various formats. Don't overwrite, and be friendly but professional.

2. Use good bond paper, nothing fancy or perfume-scented please! Make sure your printer's ribbon is dark and the printer is functioning well. Make the letter error-free.

3. Style: Use your best writing; put punch in the first sentence. Use a working title, even if it's too glib. An article about snacks for children might be called, Tricks for After-School Treats. With a snappy title, the editor understands your concept and you've got that person's attention straightaway. Your goal is to convince everyone who reads the query that your project is right. Make your sentences strong and positive.

   Outline, briefly, what you plan to cover, why your project is different, and how many words are contained in the manuscript. If photos or illustrations will be included, let that be known also.

4. In a concise manner, present your client and yourself, if appropriate, including background, experience, and qualifications for writing this manuscript.

5. Close in a businesslike manner and if you want a response, enclose a self-addressed stamped envelope.

6. Mark your calendar for three or four weeks. If you don't hear back on your query by then, it's acceptable to contact the editor for an update.

7. A word on rejection. Keep your rejection slips (if and when they come) and share them with the client. Rejection, as you know from previous writing experiences, is part of the territory and actually can help sell the material. After a number of rejections, your client or the agent will probably give some indication about the chances of the project being published or he or she might have recommendations for changes. Follow their advice, imputing your own. If you have received comments from editors, give considerable thought to them.

With the suggested changes incorporated, you should return the proposal to that specific editor along with a cover letter explaining the incorporation of their recommendations. This will not guarantee a sale, but if he or she showed enough interest to take time to write, you're definitely on the right track.

The following are two examples of query letters that have sold material. Visualize the letters on letterhead in a business-style format.

(This letter does not acknowledge the ghost.)

Date

Editor's name

Address

Dear (Editor's Name)

For most people, writing letters is up there with standing in line at the post office. It's something most would prefer to avoid. But *The Letter Book* solves this dilemma instantly. The book contains samples of letters for every need from asking for a reference to asking for unconditional love. This is the only book where a writer can plug in appropriate information without going to another source or taking time to wonder exactly what should be said.

Perfect for home, office, school, and library, *The Letter Book* is a dream come true for anyone who has been stuck for the right thing to say. In addition to containing over two hundred sample letters, there are tips on letter etiquette, grammar, and style. There is also a section on job-getting resumes.

May I send you a copy of the proposal along with three sample chapters? My curriculum vitae along with a SASE is enclosed.

Thank you for your consideration.

Sincerely,

Client's Name

(With the enclosure of a self-addressed stamped envelope.)

(This letter acknowledges the ghost.)

Date

Editor's name

Address

Dear (Agent's Name)

Not hard nor soft sell, but user-friendly sell, those red and yellow Burma-Shave road signs dotted American highways in forty-three states along millions of black-topped miles. The signs took an airy, entertaining approach to advertising when somber, dry copy was the norm. Thanks to Allan Odell, the format of advertising was changed forever.

Verse by the Side of the Road will be a nostalgic look at the origins of the Burma-Shave campaign, which spanned more than thirty years. The book will run approximately sixty thousand words and include famous slogans, how they originated, and why people just couldn't get enough of those signs of the times.

As an avid collector of Americana, especially product signs, I am the curator of thirties' memorabilia at the Los Angeles Museum of Cultural History. Professional ghostwriter Eva Shaw will be assisting in the preparation of the manuscript. The proposal is ready for review, with examples of the illustrations.

What is the all time favorite Burma-Shave sign? Impossible to tell, but this book will include hundreds that will bring a smile to the lips of every person over forty-five. Do you remember this one?

THE ANSWER TO / A MAIDEN'S / PRAYER / IS NOT A CHIN / OF STUBBY HAIR / BURMA-SHAVE.

May I send you the proposal? Enclosed is a SASE for your convenience in answering.

Thank you.

Client's name

CHAPTER
11

Selling the Book

11.1   Agents and Editors

Apples and oranges, impossible to compare the two. The literary agent works on your behalf and is paid a percentage of the advance and royalty from the book project. Editors keep their jobs and move up the corporate ladder when they select books that make a publisher money. Agents represent a book project and target the editors who might be most interested in the work.

11.2   When Should You Contact Publishers and Agents?

When is the best time to contact publishers and/or agents regarding your client's project? The minute you sign a contract with the client. Publishing is one of the slowest businesses on the face of the earth so it's never too soon as long as you can submit a professionally prepared treatment of a project.

146

Agents and publishers treat their writers with confidentiality. However, if during negotiations you are not privy to what has been sold through the agent's efforts nor provided with some of the books the publisher and/or agent's clients have published, be warned. The red flag is up for this relationship.

It is perfectly acceptable for an agent to represent many clients at the same time, just as a ghost writes for many people. The top agents are difficult to attract for those with limited experience, but until you ask you'll never know if you could be represented by that person.

As discussed before, most agents welcome an experienced ghostwriter's participation. Moreover, you can immediately and clearly define your role with a client by making yourself known to agents and publishers. On the other hand, if the client has paid you a flat rate to write the proposal, the proposal is his or her property. This is a work-for-hire arrangement and you may not receive any further business from the client. The client can submit it to any agent or publisher.

As mentioned in 10.1, The Book Proposal, you may want to include a paragraph in your contract stating that should the publisher and/or agent or client want another ghost on the project, you will receive a bonus for your work in the sale of the proposal. I've received bonuses this way a few times and it's like found money.

If the client has paid you a fee and your written agreement specifies that you will share in the advance and royalties, most likely you'll have a vote as to the terms of the publishing agreement.

147

11.3 How to Locate the Right Agent

It's a Catch-22 scheme for those who want one. One must sell to get an agent, but it's tough to sell without one. What's a ghost (and his or her client) to do? Write the finest possible query, proposal, or manuscript and its intensity will outshine the competition when an agent reads it. Surely this makes the system sound impossible to crack, but keep in mind ethical agents and publishers only make money when they sell material. A writer supplies what they need so they're constantly on the lookout for great writers with marketable material. If your client doesn't have an agent, it may be up to you to write irresistible queries to capture the interest of a potential representative for his or her literary work. Refer to the section on queries above to sell both your client and the project.

If your own bylined work is with an agent, you'll want to submit the proposal or query letter to him or her first, always with the approval of your client. You should have a good working relationship with your own agent and be able to discuss whether he or she is interested. If your agent does not handle the client's type of manuscript, then proceed as if you were looking for a new agent.

Literary Market Place, Literary Agents of North America, Writer's Market, Publisher's Weekly, regional directories of agents, referrals from publishers or agents, and referrals from friends are the options when your client desires to locate an agent. If you are in charge of locating the right person, begin the task by using consumer and investigative skills.

1. With your client, make a list of possible agents, including those agents you have a connection with. Decide whether your or the client should make the contact and the follow-up.
2. Send individual query letters to those on your list. If someone has made a recommendation refer to it in the letter.
3. Just because an agent will review your material, this does not constitute acceptance of your client's manuscript or proposal.
4. Before signing with an agent, a client may want to meet or speak with the agent.
5. Agents usually work on a project-by-project agreement. If they accept one there's usually a gentlemen's agreement that the next project will be shown to them first. There are a few agents that want exclusive agreements. This is a decision the client must make. You are a ghostwriter doing a job.
6. Once the client has signed with the agent, the agent will submit the proposal or manuscript to publishing houses.

11.4 How to Locate the Right Publisher

If your client prefers to have the book proposal or synopsis routed directly to the publisher, you may want to advise the client that:

1) Editors are overworked, many without assistants, and have piles of submissions called "slush piles." (Slush, in publishing slang, is an unsolicited manuscript.) Agented submissions are screened first and many publishers will not even accept slush, so do some checking.
2) Most editors appreciate working with reputable agents who specifically know the type of material the editor can use.
3) Many editors prefer working with agents because agents keep the negotiation on a business level.
4) While it is not impossible to sell a book without an agent, it is easier with one. A good agent will submit a manuscript to an appropriate publisher and editor. It costs time and money to make submissions and agents are cost conscious.

Follow the guidelines above. Keep in mind that if you submit the proposal or manuscript to a number of publishers, an agent may find it impossible to place unless the project is completely rewritten.

11.5   The Ghostwriter's Role in Contract Negotiation

The telephone call finally came and an offer has been made on your client's book. After jumping for joy, what happens next?

If your client is dealing through a literary agency, the

agent will provide advice on the terms of the contract. Literary agents do not accept or reject any offer for the purchase of a book; that decision is up to your client (or both of you, depending on the financial arrangement of your project).

You, as the ghost, will most likely be a resource for your client during the contract negotiation, a sounding board and a confidant. Depending on your role with your client, you may be directly involved or cemented to the sidelines.

If you haven't been involved in the sale of a book before, consider yourself lucky and learn everything you can about the process. You'll be able to pass on this insider's information to your next client.

11.6   The Anatomy of a Sale

The process can be described in steps:

1. The agent presents the book to a number of publishers.
2. Editor A immediately wants it, getting the blessing of the editorial board, and calls the agent with an offer.
3. If the agent thinks the offer is acceptable, he or she will call your client explaining the terms of the offer, including advance, royalties, rights, promotion, and expenses.

151

4. At that time, your client will probably discuss the negotiations with you and ask for professional advice.

5. The offer is either accepted or rejected.

6. If the offer is accepted, the agent contacts the publisher and a contract is forwarded to the agent and to your client for signature.

7. If the offer is rejected, the agent will counteroffer after discussing the offer clearly with your client. If your client is demanding conditions that the agent doesn't feel will be acceptable to the publisher (say, an advance five times the size of the offer), he or she will advise the client. The client and the agent will negotiate those items before the agent recontacts the publisher.

8. After the contract has been signed, a check will be forwarded to the agent. The agent will deduct his or her commission and send a check for the balance to the client. The completed book is then sent to either the publisher or the agent, depending on the agreement, or the work on the book begins.

Your role, as a professional ghostwriter, will be to assist your client who is new to publishing. Remember, too, if you are not intimately familiar with legal jargon and your client doesn't have an agent, suggest to your client that he or she seek the aid of a legal professional (in this instance it would be an entertainment or literary attorney) or the assistance of a literary agent. Some agents will accept consulting work for a flat fee or on an hourly basis.

Sometimes agents can be hired after a book deal is made, usually for a smaller commission than if they had actually placed the book with a publisher. You might ask about an hourly rate or a flat fee for this work.

CHAPTER
12

Preparing the Manuscript

12.1   The Choices for Preparation

The best way to prepare and write the manuscript is any way that accomplishes the task in the most professional and enjoyable way possible. If you are a ghostwriter still working with a manual Smith-Corona typewriter, you can make a go of it, but the bad news is that you'll be far slower than the next ghost. Today's market requires speed as well as accuracy, and neatness does count. You needn't rush out and buy an expensive computer and a laser printer, but an efficient, compatible computer system with a program that's user-friendly will speed the process.

Here are some tips when preparing the manuscript:

1. Learn to write directly on your computer, word processing system, or typewriter instead of having to write in longhand. It may feel awkward initially, but you'll save hours of time. If you don't type or key in well enough, by all means take

some classes. The one-day computer workshops are excellent. Secretarial services would love to type your manuscript, charging upwards of two dollars a page, and that can reduce your profit margin.

2. Work with your client on how the manuscript should be submitted, for draft copies as well as the final manuscript. Does he or she want to see each chapter as produced or is it more effective to submit major portions or the entire manuscript before approval? Your publishing contract will state how many hard copies (or disks) of the manuscript you must submit. It will probably be up to you (and your computer printer) to make sure that the publisher receives a clean, well-prepared copy before the deadline.

3. If your client is also working on the same computer system, you may be able to transmit the manuscript by modem or at least by exchanging computer disks. However, most seasoned ghostwriters know that a hard copy, the actual printed manuscript, is essential when editing.

4. Because your client may be extremely busy, you may be working with his or her associates or secretarial staff. You'll be expected to be a team player, and if you have the opportunity for a clerical assistant to prepare the manuscript, take advantage of it with a smile and a thank-you.

5. Depending on your agreement with your client, the research material he or she has paid you to

acquire may belong to the client. Additionally you may want to turn over all your notes, working copies, or files when you complete the project. As stated in your contract, it's highly recommended that you keep a copy of the entire, completed manuscript until the book is published; even publishing companies lose material once in a while.

6. Confidential research material is just that, confidential, and should remain so throughout the time the book is available to the public. If you've agreed not to write anything that could possibly compete with the book's topic or to use the interviews acquired during the writing process for other purposes, you will be legally bound to keep your word.

7. If your client is publishing the book on his or her own, you may be asked to submit a computer disk (or the manuscript) to a freelance editor, a copyeditor, a proofreader, or the book printer. Save a copy for yourself (unless you've contracted otherwise).

8. Depending on the agreement with your client, charge a consulting fee if you're asked to participate in meetings with his or her staff on publicity for the book, printing, promotion, or even lecture tours. If you're asked to do something above and beyond the call of a ghostwriter (teaching the client's staff the techniques described in the book for example) refer to your contract or discuss the matter with your client at once.

9. Stay in contact with all parties involved in the book's production. This keeps the enthusiasm high and helps to maintain a good working environment. Be available, but not a pest.

   It won't always be fun working on the book. If you're like most ghosts, about three-quarters of the way through any book project, you'll begin to hate the manuscript. As bliss turns to agony, take heart because that's a good sign. You're doing your job. When writing becomes painful, persevere and complete the project. Such tenacity will set your work apart from that of other would-be ghosts. Become known as the ghostwriter who finishes all the books and projects you start.

10. Keep a sense of humor. Work on various other projects, if possible, while ghosting one client's book, and you won't get overly tired of the topic. And know that with each book completed your resume will become more credible.

12.2 The Mechanics of Format

If you've already outlined the book, it's time to begin writing. If you haven't outlined the book, it's still possible to write it. But without a map to guide you through the process, you can be guaranteed severe frustration. (See chapter 7 for preparation and methods of outlining.)

You may also want to secure a copy of David L. Carroll's

How to Prepare Your Manuscript for A Publisher (Paragon House, 1988) for a complete review of the how-tos.

Here's what you need to know about the mechanics of preparing the manuscript:

1. Print or type the final copy of your manuscript on sturdy bond paper. Many hands will touch it and while sixteen-pound bond is more economical, it will not withstand the wear that a manuscript is submitted to during the editing process. Never use erasable bond; it smears the print on the page and it's a sign of a novice. Use $8^{1}/_{2}$-by-11, unless you clear it first with your publisher.

2. The use of continuous paper for your computer is fine, but make sure to remove the perforated guides and separate the manuscript into pages before submitting it to a publisher. If you're using a computer, double-check the page breaks so you don't inadvertently leave a title on one page with the text appearing (untitled) on the next.

3. Check your printer or typewriter ribbon before you begin and also halfway through the printing process. Make sure that the ribbon is dark and the print is clear. Editors, notoriously, have tired eyes and you can promote good relations with this one tip alone.

4. The manuscript should be formatted in double-spaced lines.

5. If you have end notes, make sure your computer prints them on the same page.

6. Set margins at least one inch all around the page. Some editors prefer $1^1/_4$ inches. Depending on your print font, you should print about 250 words per page.

7. Indent all paragraphs five spaces.

8. Chose a print style that is easy to read such as sans serif or Roman. Italic print is not acceptable nor is dot matrix because it's hard to read and doesn't photocopy well.

9. If you plan to include graphs, drawings, or illustrations within the manuscript, let the editor know what is coming and where, such as: [Ed: Drawing 8.2 to be included here.]. Number all art and send it to the editor in a separate package along with a caption manuscript (if needed) also double-spaced.

10. If you have sidebars that you plan to have boxed, let your editor know. The placement of the sidebar will be a decision, most likely, for the book designer, but it's up to the ghostwriter and client to provide information. You may want to write: [Ed: Sidebar as follows should be a box in a thick line as discussed. Sidebar to go here.].

11. Center all chapter titles.

12. Start chapters one-third of the way down the page.

13. Consecutively number all pages. If you absolutely see no alternative but to add a page, it is acceptable to page with a letter after the page number, such as page 212, followed by page 212A. This is a situation that might occur if you're typing the

manuscript, find a mistake, and decide the correction requires additional room, or if you need to make a crucial addition without reprinting the manuscript.

14. While your publisher pays someone to check spelling, it improves your credibility to turn in a 98 percent error-free manuscript. Run the manuscript through the spell-checking program on your computer even if you're a certifiable marvel at words. Computer spell checks only find misspelled words . . . if you've inserted "that" instead of the correct word "than," it's up to a human to discover the flaw.

    You may want to enlist a friend or pay someone to proofread your manuscript if you have trouble spotting errors.

15. The "slug," your client's name (with pseudonym in parentheses) and key word from the title, should appear on every page. Some ghosts prefer the page number at the bottom, others place it at the top. Check with your publisher if in doubt.

16. If your client is using a pen name, his or her legal name must appear on the manuscript, normally in the upper right-hand corner of the first page. If your client is not crediting you, the ghost, with any part of the book, remember that when you prepare the manuscript.

17. Correct typing errors neatly. If you have more than two corrections on a page, retype or reprint that page. After all that attention to detail you find

you've missed a word, it's acceptable *once in a while* to insert it between two typed words above the sentence.

18. Estimate the correct number of words in the manuscript and type that on the front page. Don't try to mislead publishers . . . remember, words are their business.

    To estimate words, count the number of words on a typical page, multiply that by the number of pages. Variations occur so you may want to count a few pages, get an average, then multiply that number by the total number of pages. The number of words on a page is determined by the printer font size and the type of words. If you're working on a highly scientific manual for space-age medicine, for example, you'll have longer words than if you're writing a geography book for second graders.

    With some word processing programs and the use of their word counter (such as with Word-Perfect 5.0) there may be a variation between the number of words when counted through the spell check and counted by the word counter. Depending on your length and format, this may be a difference of a thousand or so.

19. Do not staple or bind the manuscript when you submit it to the publisher, unless you get the go-ahead to do so. However, clients often appreciate having the drafts of the book bound in a plastic spiral notebook with clear plastic covers.

20. At the end of the manuscript, type "End" or, as some writers prefer, ###.

21. When mailing a manuscript to the client or a publisher, send it first class and certify it with a return receipt required, if peace of mind is high on your list. An express mail service is fast, reliable, and efficient and for a small sum they will pick up the package at your office plus verify delivery. Always wrap the manuscript securely; use a sturdy box, manuscript box, or an envelope that has a plastic bubble liner. They are good investments.

12.3 The Final Phase: Writing the Manuscript

Depending on your working relationship with your client, he or she will probably not see the manuscript until you've written it and worked it through two or three times. These are *your* working drafts. Strive for no more than three printed drafts whether you're working on a computer or a typewriter. Although you may work through the material a number of times, only print as many drafts as you actually require; printing takes time and paper is expensive.

Go back and review the myth of writer's block if you hit a stumbling point in preparation for the manuscript. Sometimes the hardest chapter to write is the first, but forge ahead knowing you can always return and rewrite once you feel the texture and tone of the manuscript. To ease the writing process, review all your research material, detailed outline, and assorted notes the day before you're scheduled to begin writing and throughout the process. Reading the notes before bed might help your subconscious format the text. You may want to repeat this procedure nightly.

Depend heavily on your detailed chapter outline, but don't be afraid to alter it (with your client's approval or suggestions) as you go along. The outline is your guide. You may want to update it so that when the book is complete, you have the basis for a table of contents.

If working with a computer program, such as Word-Perfect 5.0, utilize the "switch" screen function (Shift F3) to write material on two documents (Doc) files. Pull the manuscript up on Doc 1, the outline on Doc 2, and coordinate the writing and outline review with ease.

When working on the first draft, don't labor over any topic. Let your mind and your fingers move freely. Get it written. Choose your words with care but take the concepts from your outline and put them into sentences your reader can comprehend. There's no great mystery here . . . write the book or article reflecting your client's word patterns with skill and an eye on practicality because you're in the business of ghostwriting. Sure there will be parts of the project you know you can write better—that's what second drafts are for . . . just get the words down, then edit.

When you produce the manuscript from the detailed chapter outline, read it through making changes on the copy you're working from. But as much as you'd like to share this first go-through with your client, hold back. The next step is significant to the process.

Allow the manuscript to chill. This step, according to pro ghosts, saves considerable embarrassment. After a day, a week, or a month, depending on your deadline for the first draft, go back and read the manuscript through again. Your mind will be sharper, the material will have a freshness, and you'll be able to correct, change, remedy, and create with a clearer eye to particulars. Be sure to read as if you're the client and the editor.

Your first draft is bound to look very messy; that's okay. However, make your corrections and changes in legible style so that you can discuss them with your client; it's always shocking not to be able to read your own writing. Making changes in a pen of a different shade than your printer will speed the process.

As you go through the manuscript and find areas that need attention, make an X in the margin, highlight it with a yellow marker, and/or fold the corner of the page down so you can return and make the necessary adjustment.

While making additions on the draft, you may want to cut and paste (especially if you're not working on a computer). Physically take a paragraph from one page, cut it out, and paste it onto another section. Your next step may be to photocopy that page and make any necessary changes.

If at any point you feel unsure of how a client might

discuss what you've written, consult with him or her, listen to the tapes of your work sessions, and/or read over the previously written material to get once again a feel of his or her word pattern. You may not be paid to flatter your client totally at all times, but it's essential that you capture the tone of his or her words throughout the manuscript. That's a ghost's job.

After you've input the modifications, submit a copy to your client with a deadline for the return. Explain it is a rough draft and write Working Copy or Draft in bold letters on top of the manuscript.

During the time that your client is reviewing the manuscript, you may be working through various parts that need attention. Confer with your client, have a trusted associate review the manuscript to look for discrepancies or omissions, then continue with your research. It's always amazing what turns up and must be included when you think you've written it all.

Once you've met to discuss and incorporate changes, make the changes and again allow the manuscript to chill. I recommend a minimum of a week. Then confer again before you input the changes.

Always keep busy with other work while the manuscript is being review by the client. Otherwise depression can set in and you may begin doubting your own creativity. When you're at the point of producing the first draft, line up the next project, if one isn't waiting. When you complete the second and final draft for your client, you should then begin your next project. It's a wise ghost who works on many projects at one time . . . the business is filled with available time slots that need to be filled with work for pay.

Review the manuscript, make changes, and print the final copy. Photocopy (or print) a copy for yourself and one for your client, or duplicate your computer disk. After he or she has approved the final copy, submit the original (and perhaps one copy) to the publisher or agent.

If you've worked closely with your client and publisher, minor changes will be all that are required. For extensive changes that are needed because of a client's indecision or inclusion of new research or material, fall back on the paragraph in your contract stating the fees for lengthy revisions—unless of course, you were off the mark.

12.4   Cover Copy, Author's Note

It may be your privilege to write the blurb for the back of the book, the short bio for your client, acknowledgments, author's dedication, and anything else the client feels is essential for the book. Depending on who is asked to write the foreword or introduction, you, as a ghost, may write everything in the book. As you begin any project, discuss the need for this material with your client. Make the material a part of your drafts.

While working on the manuscript, keep these extras in mind and your brain will begin to format what you'll say. For many clients these sections are almost as important as the entire text of their book because they are a personal reflection of the client as a flesh-and-blood human being.

Be gracious to everyone and generous with praise for others who have helped on the book. And if your client wants to heap you with appreciation (even if the world isn't to know that you wrote the book), accept it all with a warm smile. Your reputation will be enhanced with every totally satisfied customer and you *can* take that to the bank.

12.5   How Long Does It Take to Ghost a Book?

How much time should you estimate to write a book? That depends on your speed as a writer. Some ghosts produce six good pages a day and feel accomplished. Others only feel successful when they've written four to six thousand words a day. As a ghost, it's your business to produce words in a timely, entertaining, and efficient manner.

If you must spend twenty hours to write a one-thousand-word article, charging twenty cents a word, your hourly rate is well below prosperity level. There is a however here, because if that one-thousand-word article is destined to lead to regular, weekly work that is handsomely rewarded, then your twenty-hour investment is well worth it.

The average ghost can write a book-length manuscript (that does not require extensive research or interviewing) in three to six months. You may have to work nights, evenings, and when everyone you know in the entire world is on vacation, but you'll also have the pleasure of working at your own business, on your own schedule, on your own time, and for your own future.

As you become familiar with the client's word pattern, use of adjectives and/or expletives, the process will become second nature. Like anything else ghostwriting requires a period of learning . . . if everyone could do it, we'd be out of business.

Generally it's in your best interest as a ghost to work as quickly as possible while keeping quality high. It's not easy. You may be required to become a genius at time management, a guru of juggling family and work responsibilities, plus a veritable whiz at writing. But with dedication, thoroughness, and time, you can and will become a respected *and* requested ghostwriter.

CHAPTER
13

Ghostwriting Is a Craft

13.1   Who's Who of Ghostwriting

Ghostwriting can't be learned overnight; there are no quick and easy lessons. And so far science hasn't perfected an inoculation that turns even the most creative writer into a skilled ghost.

The learning concept of how to become a money-making ghostwriter is outlined in this book, but you can only read so much. It is now time to take your show on the road and if you have the initiative and perseverance, you will succeed.

Success, however, isn't always spelled with dollar signs. It's knowing within your deepest self that you're satisfied with your approach to life. Your creative endeavors are appreciated (and well paid for) and you wake each day with joyful anticipation knowing you're going to work. And since there is money to be made as a ghost, that alone can go a long way to increase your joy of life.

In a recent article in the *Wall Street Journal* ghostwriting was discussed as a growth industry. According to the article publishers are infatuated with ghostwritten books with celebrity and business leaders as the authors. Sure they have a short shelf life, but they sell incredibly well. Five of the top twenty-five best-sellers of the 1980s were ghosted as-told-to books. The newspaper article recounts that *Iacocca: An Autobiography*, again by pro ghost William Novak, has sold more copies since its publication in 1984 than any other nonfiction book in history, except for a few reference volumes, the Bible, and Betty Crocker's cookbooks. There's a market for your work. Novak did it . . . and so can you.

How do your contemporaries approach their craft of ghostwriting? Here are some quotes from other professionals, plus suggestions on making the most of your ability, and some differences of opinion.

CHARLES LEERHSEN, *Trump: Surviving at the Top* (with Donald Trump), was recently accused of "prostituting his talents." His rebuttal? "Not at all . . . I felt rich." Sources say Leerhsen received no royalties, but a fee in the mid-six-figures category.

YVONNE DUNLEAVY, *The Happy Hooker* (with Xaviera Hollander), says that ghostwriting is excellent mental exercise: "It frees your concentration, buys time, and keeps your writing mind active and alert. You're less likely to get blocked or make as many false starts. Ghosting can build confidence. It lets you know you have another skill." Dunleavy encourages simultaneously writing as a ghost and on your own work: "Fiction is art and comes from emotion; ghosting is craft and comes from information."

SAMM SINCLAIR BAKER, coauthor with Irwin Stillman of *The Doctor's Quick Weight Loss Diet* and with Herman Tarnower on *The Complete Scarsdale Medical Diet*, explains, "No partnership is any good that isn't fifty-fifty." He insists that an *and* and a fifty-fifty royalty be arranged on all his books. "Otherwise, the expert is saying the writer is inferior."

MARTIN MAYER, who wrote among other books Sol Linowitz's *The Making of a Public Man*, doesn't need his name on the cover to feel complete. And that's the reason you may not recognize it: "I see my name on the covers of enough books. My contribution is strictly a technical one. To write the book that person would write if he could write a book." Mayer is quick to point out that he's not responsible for opinions and/or judgments in the book: "It's not *my* book."

SANDRA HARMON, *Elvis and Me* (with Priscilla Presley), feels that the hardest part is establishing a common ground: "Getting close to the person and getting them to trust you, then putting all the elements together and speaking in the voice of that person" is the essence of ghostwriting.

KENNETH TURAN, *Call Me Anna: The Autobiography of Patty Duke*, says, "If you do it just for the money, you're in trouble. I've had friends who wrote books for money and it was like working in a butcher shop."

VICKI LINDNER, the ghostwriter of *Cheryl Tiegs: The Way to Natural Beauty* and other collaborated or ghost-written books plus scores of novels under her own byline, cautions that the celebrity may not be familiar with how a writer works nor have a sense of how useful a skilled ghost can be: "They think all they have to do is provide the information. Cheryl Tiegs called me 'someone who did research for the book.' " But Lindner continues, "On the other hand, everyone knows Tiegs didn't write the book. And I came into contact with a great many things I wouldn't have otherwise. New experiences gave me new metaphors and a new reality, revitalizing my fiction."

LEONARD FELDER, the author of *Learning to Love Forever* (with psychotherapist Adalaide Bry) and many articles and books, reminds ghosts, "Under no circumstances should you as a collaborator let your name be omitted from the cover or title page. Unless your name appears in both places, it will not be included on the library catalogue card or in *Books in Print*. In order to build your career and reputation, you will need to spell out in advance, in your agreement, that your name must appear on the title page and cover or jacket, even if it's in smaller type."

WILLIAM PROCTOR, cowriter with Pat Boone, Art Linkletter, Kenneth Cooper, and others, is a veteran in the ghost field and is fairly loose about byline credits: "My druthers are to have my name on the book, but it's just more professional not to create a fuss. After all, please buy the book for the expert, not for me."

LINDA BIRD FRANCHKE, who has written with Rosalynn Carter and Geraldine Ferraro, says, "A key to making a project work is capturing the language of the celebrity. When I did Rosalynn Carter, I typed with a

Southern accent. When I did Geraldine Ferraro, I wrote more in Queens brusque."

The aforementioned WILLIAM NOVAK, called by *Newsweek* magazine "The King of Ghosts," and ghostwriter of Tip O'Neill's *Speaker of the House* besides *Iacocca* and *My Turn*, reveals that after doing exhaustive research on a client, including interviews with family members, friends, and business associates, he makes lists of questions to ask the celebrity. Personally, he says, "I don't fool myself into thinking that *my* books are best-sellers. The celebrities are the selling point."

Will your name be the next on the list of notables who write for the movers and shakers of our time? All it takes is enterprise, ambition, and a talent for writing in a client's voice . . . only better.

If your occupation as well as your preoccupation is writing, and if you're addicted to the pleasure of eating, living, and traveling well, ghostwriting is the only game in town.

APPENDIX
A

Ghostwriter's Reference Source

T HE following books range from essential (*Literary Market Place* and *Writer's Market*) to nice to have for reference (*How to Write Irresistible Query Letters*). They are the books I recommend to beginning ghosts and to those who have been in the business and want to add to their personal library. Keep in mind that some of the books do just as well on your public library shelf as they do in your office, so I've divided the list that way. If you find you're using the library's reference copy of a book time and again, it's smarter to buy one. Save the receipt . . . it's a tax deduction.

If you're a medical ghostwriter, you'll need specialized books. If you ghost for an accountant or a anthropologist, you'll require different references.

The following will get you started:

In Your Office Library

Carroll, David L. *How to Prepare Your Manuscript For A Publisher*. New York, N.Y.: Paragon House, 1988. Six dollars. This book will tell you everything you need to know about preparing a professional manuscript.

Poynter, Dan. *The Self-Publishing Manual*. Santa Barbara, Calif.: Para Publishing, 1989. About twenty dollars. This is the ultimate answer book if your client wants to self-publish. It's worth reading to gain an appreciation of what he or she will have to go through to get the book out. Also, as a ghost, you'll be more helpful if you know what a book printer needs and can advise the client on the system even in the discussion stage of your relationship.

Telephone book (free for the asking). Your public library probably has most telephone books from large metropolitan areas. You can obtain ones from other areas for a nominal fee by contacting your phone company.

AT&T Toll-Free 800 Directory. Puts you in touch with companies and resource contacts who do business with toll-free 800 numbers. About ten dollars.

Writer's Digest Magazine, Writer's Digest Books. Cincinnati, Ohio. Monthly. About eighteen dollars a year. The May 1990 issue features writers' conferences throughout the country. The magazine's articles tend to be basic, but the classified section and information about publishers and magazines are invaluable. The classifieds also have periodic listings from clients looking for ghostwriters and collaborators. Read it for those reasons alone.

Writer's Market, Writer's Digest Books. Cincinnati, Ohio. Annual. About twenty-four dollars, sometimes less at discount and membership stores. Lists most of the book and magazine publishers in the United States and some in Canada with approximately four thousand annotations. The book, obviously, takes time to write and some information is outdated before it even goes to press. This is also true with *Writer's Handbook* (see below). Double-check with publisher and magazine editors for verification, if necessary. This is a good source for contests, agents, syndicates, and general writing information.

In addition you'll need a good desk-size dictionary . . . the computer's spell check might not have the word you need. I prefer the fat, small, paperback *Webster's New World Dictionary* yet I also have a very large unabridged dictionary that I keep on the office shelf. A thesaurus, an almanac, and an atlas will all come in handy for obvious reasons.

If you own or can get a secondhand set of encyclopedias, they're a good investment. Sometimes you just need a tidbit of information. There are paperback one-book editions such as *The Concise Columbia Encyclopedia* that might be a helpful reference source, too.

In the public library:

Books in Print. Eight volume set about $316. This is the definitive work by topic, title, and author of books that are available. *The* source if you want to check on other books on your proposed topic, books with the same name as yours, books written that compete with yours and/or books written by your client (with the help of another ghost).

Cool, Lisa Collier. *How to Write Irresistible Query Letters*. Cincinnati, Ohio: Writer's Digest Books, 1987. About eleven dollars. Probably the best book on the market on writing brilliant query letters. About twenty sample queries to stimulate your own golden queries.

Larson, Michael. *How to Write a Book Proposal*. Cincinnati, Ohio: Writer's Digest Books, 1986. About eleven dollars. Not all editors and agents agree on Larson's format, but he does provide sound information on workable and marketable ways to write proposals.

Horowitz, Lois. *A Writer's Guide to Research*. Cincinnati, Ohio: Writer's Digest Books, 1986. About ten dollars. A good reference source if you need direction or a refresher course on how to obtain information quickly and accurately.

Literary Market Place. About $110. A national listing of all book and magazine publishing sources, trade publications, industry associations, publishers' toll-free telephone numbers, book manufacturers and printers, editorial services, and a listing of agents with books that they've represented. There is also an *International Literary Market Place*.

Publishers Weekly, New York. About eighty dollars a year. Brings you up-to-the-minute information on who's buying what and plenty of inside scoop on the publishing industry. It also has book reviews and a help-wanted section.

The Reader's Guide to Periodic Literature. About $150 per volume. In book, microfiche, and computerized form, a listing by year (and month for more recent material) of popular magazines published in the United States. Listed by topic.

Schwarz, Ted. *Time Management For Writers*. Cincinnati, Ohio: Writer's Digest Books, 1988. About eleven dollars. A book to help any writer organize his or her time effectively. Great tips whether you're a novice or an old pro.

Writer's Handbook. Boston, Mass. The Writer, Inc. Annual. About thirty dollars. A competitor to *Writer's Market* with a slightly more serious outlook on writing. Included in the handbook are how-to-write and inspirational articles and a listing of twenty-five hundred markets for work.

APPENDIX
B

*How to Get Information
for the Asking*

• Access library computer data searches such as *The
Reader's Guide to Periodic Literature.*

• Periodicals like the *Journal of the American Medical
Association,* the *New York Times,* and the *Los Angeles
Times* are indexed for ease in locating information.

• Almanacs, dictionaries, directories, and the magazines that are kept on file in the library.

• Your public library may not have detailed information you require on every project. However, uni-
versities, colleges, medical centers, museums, local
governments, government offices, and research centers
(sometimes special approval is required, sometimes a
small deposit) will allow the public to use their resources.

• Your client may have access to private libraries
such as a medical library at a hospital.

• As a resident of a town with a state-supported
college or university, you may be able to obtain a
library card. There may be a fee but that's a business

expense (if you use the library for business) and deductible.

• The United States Government (and the Government Printing Office, Washington, D.C. 20401, 202/275–2051) is another gold mine of free or almost free information. Get on their mailing list.

• National newspapers such as the *Wall Street Journal* and *USA Today* are excellent sources of statistics and trends. All the Who's Who books provide facts and clues to other sources, possibly unlocking the information you so desperately need.

• There are more public relations companies, foundations, institutes, and support groups than a mind can fathom. Smart ghosts access information through these associations and most of it is free for the asking. The organizations provide technical and lay information, photos, telephone numbers of experts, facts, and statistics.

• Manufacturing companies, food producers and growers, chain stores, lobbies, schools, and societies have public information/consumer service sections eager to assist a ghostwriter. It might take a few phone calls, but the research and investigation process will be well worth the trouble.

• If you need photos, names of experts to interview, brochures, or recommended reading ask the nonprofit organization, manufacturers, anyone who you think might have the information. Most likely you'll be inundated with material, but that's okay. It's better to have too much than too little. When using free material always credit the organization that supplied it.

• If you become specialized in ghostwriting a particular topic you may want to ask that your name be added to the mailing list of the journals in this area, such as the newsletter published by The National Kidney Foundation. Within its pages you might read about upcoming procedures or obtain the name of a scientist developing a new treatment. Items like these could tie in nicely with a new project.

APPENDIX
C

Writers' Organizations

CURRENTLY there's no American Society of Ghost-writers yet you'll benefit by joining one of the writers' networks. Write for information and select the one that's best for you.

This list, keep in mind, is not complete. For more writers' associations, refer to the *Encyclopedia of Associations*, Gale Research Company, available at most libraries. It contains information on myriad writers groups from topics as varied as bowling to UFOs.

- AMERICAN MEDICAL WRITERS
  ASSOCIATION
  9650 Rockville Pike
  Bethesda, MD 20814

- AMERICAN SOCIETY OF JOURNALISTS
  AND AUTHORS, INC.
  1501 Broadway, Suite 1907,
  New York, NY 10036

- THE AUTHORS LEAGUE OF AMERICA
  234 W. 44th Street
  New York, NY 10036

- MYSTERY WRITERS OF AMERICA, INC.
  236 W. 27th Street
  New York, NY 10001

- NATIONAL ASSOCIATION OF SCIENCE
  WRITERS, INC.
  P.O. Box 294
  Greenlawn, NY 11740

- THE NATIONAL WRITERS CLUB
  1450 S. Havana, Suite 620
  Aurora, CO 80012

- NATIONAL WRITERS UNION
  13 Astor Place, 7th Floor
  New York, NY 10003

- OUTDOOR WRITERS ASSOCIATION
  2017 Cato Ave., Suite 101
  State College, PA 16801

- PEN AMERICAN CENTER
  568 Broadway
  New York, NY 10012

- ROMANCE WRITERS OF AMERICA
  5206 FM 1960 West, #208
  Houston, TX 77069

- SCIENCE FICTION WRITERS OF AMERICA
  P.O. Box 4236
  West Columbia, SC 29171

- SOCIETY FOR TECHNICAL
  COMMUNICATION
  815 15th Street NW
  Washington, D.C. 20005

- WESTERN WRITERS OF AMERICA
  1753 Victoria
  Sheridan, WY 82801

- WRITERS GUILD OF AMERICA, EAST, INC.
  555 W. 57th Street
  New York, NY 10019

- WRITERS GUILD OF AMERICA, WEST, INC.
  8455 Beverly Blvd.
  Los Angeles, CA 90048

About the Author

Eva Shaw is a professional ghostwriter who has published more than one thousand books, magazine articles, newspaper columns, and speeches under her clients' bylines, plus many books and articles on which her own name appears.

A resident of Carlsbad, California, Shaw says, "Ghostwriting is the best of all writing worlds—you can make a handsome living, and it's constantly a challenge. It's pleasure and money."